WELIGAMA

EMILY DOBBS

WELIGAMA

RECIPES FROM SRI LANKA

EMILY DOBBS

SEVEN DIALS

For Marie

Contents

Introduction

In the late 1980s my uncle went on holiday to Sri Lanka, and never came back. He became very influential in the tourist industry, buying one of the first boutique hotels on the island, founding the charity 'Adopt Sri Lanka' during the tsunami in 2004 and setting up the Galle Literary festival in 2007.

He lives on Taprobane Island – a strip of jungle perched on rocks with an old white house – off Weligama Bay. My family and I first went to visit him 15 years ago when Sri Lanka was in the midst of civil war. We seemed to be the only tourists and you weren't allowed to travel north of Colombo. I remember that smack of hot, humid air with the strong, musty scent of the tropics when I stepped off the plane. I still look forward to that moment when I visit now. I instantly feel at home in Sri Lanka.

Back then, there wasn't a motorway and it would take a whole day to get to Galle from Colombo airport, travelling on the rusty red broken-down steam train, with its many cases of 'engine trouble'. My sister and I loved it, tap water wasn't safe to drink so it was a free pass to guzzle Sprite and Coca-Cola from those iconic glass bottles with thick red straws.

Rising at dawn, we'd watch the pink sunrises from Taprobane Island with my grandmother, who would tell us stories of her childhood growing up in Australia.

I remember that smack of hot, humid air with the strong, must scent of the tropics when I stepped off the plane.

We would listen while looking out over a calm turquoise sea with multi-coloured wooden fishing boats bobbing peacefully against a pearly grey morning mist.

Copying the locals, we kids delighted in eating curry with our right hand instead of using a fork and drinking pumpkin-coloured coconuts 'thambili' straight off the palm tree. I remember being made to do homework to the sound of monks chanting their afternoon prayers during monsoon. Every morning we swallowed bitter, chalky malaria pills hidden in thick, sweet MD brand strawberry jam before a breakfast of imported Marmite and 'banis' – Sri Lankan sweet bread – together with fresh tropical fruit, sambols and string hoppers.

As I got older, I often thought that food in London lacked the vibrancy, colour and freshness of Sri Lankan cooking. I couldn't understand why it was so difficult to find good-quality Sri Lankan food like you could Italian food. It simply wasn't a popular or understood cuisine in the West.

My favourite Italian restaurant is the River Café in Hammersmith. I love everything about that place from the garden overlooking the Thames to their easy-to-use, timeless cookbooks. Rose Gray, one of the co-founders of the restaurant, was friendly with my uncle and grandmother, having cooked at the Galle Literary festival. She loved Sri Lanka and loved painting it too. I began to imagine a Sri Lankan River Café. I would call it Weligama; I loved the name – a reminder of childhood memories on Taprobane Island – and it sounded warm and welcoming. Playful.

I am a creative and have never been text-book 'cheffy'. The thought process from developing a recipe to the final plating of a dish is similar to the work of a painting or sculpture. Like an artist, you experiment with different ingredients to create flavour combinations, and the little notebook you write down recipe ideas in is your sketchbook.

At art school, I would mix spices with egg yolk, creating pastes to paint with. I've always loved to experiment, whether it be in a studio or a kitchen. My fascination with spices began to evolve; I loved the smells, earthy colours and the organic nature of working with them. Pouring vinegar on to the canvas so that it would erode and spoil. I loved to paint the waves of the sea; I would go to Brighton and sit on the pebbles overlooking the crashing surf, reminiscing about Mirissa Beach in south Sri Lanka.

My first cooking job was a bit random and spontaneous: it was on a ranch in Wyoming. I loved the freedom of cooking whatever I wanted. I began to cook curries on Thursdays,

My fascination with spices began to flourish; I loved the smells, earthy colours and the organic nature of working with them.

I loved to paint the waves of the sea; I would go to Brighton and sit on the pebbles overlooking the crashing surf, reminiscing about Mirissa Beach in south Sri Lanka.

introducing a new one each week inspired by my grandmother, who emailed me recipes she had learnt from living in Delhi in the 50s. The first curry I ever learnt to make is in this book on page 130.

When I came back to the UK, I started work at the Dock Kitchen, which opened my eyes to beautiful produce. I had never before seen the bright pink-and-white casing of Borlotti beans or the delicate stripes of a Castelfranco raddichio. My job was to pick fresh elderflowers and nettles alongside the canal, then pod peas in the sun on the terrace.

From there I went to Ducksoup in Soho. There is such an energy and buzz in that part of London and I came to know all the little local shops, buying fresh pasta from Camisa on Old Compton Street; fish sauce and curry leaves from Chinatown; and borrowing olive oil from Quo Vadis when we ran out.

Throughout working in busy London restaurants, I was still secretly obsessed with Sri Lankan food; I bought every Sri Lankan cookbook I could find and taught myself how to cook it at home. I found a recipe for egg hoppers that looked unlike anything I had ever seen before and that excited me. Having read they were notoriously difficult to make I set myself a challenge. I liked the idea but wanted to develop it into something new and original. At the time, I was struggling with my health and needed a distraction.

I spent ages testing them: either they would stick to the pan or flop out like limp, soggy pancakes. Frustrated, but stubborn, I ran around South Harrow,

Tooting Broadway and Southall markets for months asking for tips on how to cook a hopper. Always met with the same response: a frown and a, 'Miss, even my mother can't make hoppers!'

Finally, after months of failures and late-night hopper floppers, I finally had it sussed. The pan had to be not too hot, not too cold: the Goldilocks temperature. I discovered a secret ingredient and came up with my own fool-proof recipe (page 26). Overcome with excitement, I bought a second-hand camping stove and, armed with my hopper gear, I demonstrated my creation to the owners of Hatch in Homerton.

They loved it and said I could do a pop-up on Sundays. I had no signage. No business plan. No money. To top it off, nobody knew what they were. So I wrote a description of how to eat them. 'They are nice', I wrote in chalk.

In Sri Lanka, hoppers are as basic as sliced white bread. I wanted to liven them up, so I created different varieties to make them fun and interesting: the mini egg hopper; the hopper whopper; and my cult Weligama egg hopper with pol sambol, seeni sambol, kirry hoddy dipping sauce, lime and peanuts. A 'flavour bomb' designed to be rolled up and eaten with your hands, like a taco, Weligama hoppers became the modern, updated egg hopper. The *Evening Standard* described them as 'Utterly fantastic, a cult hit' and that I was 'Hopping mad'.

My hopper stall, Weligama, opened in May 2015, followed by Hoppers restaurant on Frith Street, central London that October. Sri Lankan food had finally caught the attention of the London food scene and was trending.

Trading at markets provided me with a solid platform to find my voice in food and evolve as a cook, but I evolved even more while writing this book. I took some time out from the stall and spent it researching Sri Lankan food and the country to further develop my style of cooking. At first, I was adamant every ingredient had to be authentic – stressing out if I couldn't find dill seed. Over time, I found it best to work with the seasons and make use of whatever was available in the UK. Cooking seasonally not only makes the ingredient more special and unique, it sets a boundary that can sharpen your creativity as your choice for produce is limited, giving you a framework and structure.

My cooking is influenced and inspired by the people with whom I've worked and the places I've explored. I find it fascinating going back to the roots of production, observing how cinnamon is produced, tea picked and rice harvested. I stick with Asian influences while using ingredients readily available in the UK. Unlike traditional Sri Lankan cooking, I cook meat slowly and fish fast. I reduce the amount of spice whilst keeping it fresh with lots of lime juice and fresh herbs. I like knowing where things come from by supporting small business and their produce. Everything has a story.

My recipes are not a set of rules but guidelines. 'Taste as you go' is my main suggestion, together with:

- **Practise mise en place** – *prep all your ingredients before you start and have an organised and clean set up. You will feel calmer and more zen. If you are feeling good your food will taste good.*

- **Read the recipe beforehand** – *so you know you have all the right ingredients and tools with which to start. There might be an element you need to make in advance, for example buffalo labneh or chilli butter.*

- **Don't stress if you don't have all the ingredients** – *you can often swap one for something else (see the substitution table on page 23).*

- **Don't go too crazy with spices** – *you can get a bit distracted grating a nutmeg, but too much and your teeth will go numb or you will hallucinate!*

- **Don't panic!** – *If something f**ks up, let your guests join in – get everyone involved. Invite your kids to crack the eggs and your great-aunt to pick herbs.*

Above all, relax, be inventive, inquisitive and instinctive rather than prude and exact. Remember that cooking, plating and sharing food is a way of expressing oneself, and connecting to others. It frees the mind yet connects the soul. Learning to cook is a lifelong journey and every enthusiast should remain humble and hungry to learn more. Keep exploring, and don't be afraid to be different and try something new.

Sri Lankan sample menus

A proper Sri Lankan meal will consist of every taste, colour and texture sensation – sweet, salty, bitter, spicy, crunchy, creamy, wet, dry, fresh and raw. These elements are brought together in harmony by soulful rice, a staple food in Sri Lanka, accompanied by a variety of curries all served at once; something crunchy like poppadoms or fried bitter gourd; a cooked salad (known as mallum) and a selection of sambols and pickle, sometimes known as 'rice pullers'.

Here are some seasonal menu suggestions for 4–6 people.

A proper Sri Lankan meal will consist of every taste, colour and texture sensation

SPRING
Lamb neck's curry (see Venison curry – page 82)
Fried mackerel curry (see Squid curry – page 100)
Egg curry (page 34)
Raw asparagus and mint sambol (page 157)
Wild mushrooms with chilli, arrack and yoghurt (page 152)

SUMMER
Rabbit curry (page 86)
Squid curry (page 100)
Tomato Curry (page 40)
Samphire, mango and lime sambol (page 157)
Papaya, radish, buffalo curd and chilli salad (page 145)

AUTUMN
Chicken curry (page 86)
Pumpkin curry (page 128)
Fried leeks with crispy onions (page 162)
Cabbage mallum, using turnip tops (page 160)

WINTER
Beef curry (page 93)
Cabbage Mallum (page 160)
Sweet potato curry (page 121)
Beetroot curry (page 118)
Carrot and orange sambol (page 156)

Sri Lankan ingredients

Sri Lanka's abundance of exotic vegetables, red rice, healing spices, Ceylon tea, coconut and buffalo yoghurt equals a diet that is healthy, nutritious and hugely satisfying. Vivid in color, vibrancy, richness and warmth and naturally lactose/gluten free. All Serendip. By chance. Serendip is the ancient name of Sri Lanka, meaning Serendipity: *'the occurrence and development of events by chance in a happy or beneficial way.'*

I love exploring Asian market arounds London on the hunt for typical Sri Lankan produce. A trip to Chinatown, South Harrow, Tooting, east London and Brixton is as inspiring as a quick holiday, if only for the big bunches of coriander with their roots intact. A fraction of the price and way more flavour than what is on offer from the supermarket. I encourage you to seek out any Asian markets near you – it's much cheaper and more characteristic than the average supermarket.

Below is a list of a few online shops I use and what they are good for, and over the next few pages you'll find descriptions of some of my most-used Sri Lankan ingredients.

ocado.com
rose water and oritz anchovies

amazon.co.uk
Bulk order chaokoh coconut milk, Por Kwan tamarind paste, arrack, Ceylon cinnamon, ground cardamom, nuts, desiccated coconut

asiancookshop.com
Red rice flour, pandan etc. coconut vinegar, mustard oil, fresh fenugreek

I. Spices

The most commonly used 'Lankan' spices are coriander seed, cumin seed, fenugreek, cinnamon, clove, chili, fennel seed, turmeric, green cardamom, nutmeg and black mustard seed. As long as these are in your cupboard, with vast tins of coconut milk, dried anchovies as substitutes for maldive fish and a good few limes, you are pretty set.

Spices should always be bought whole and kept away from direct light and heat. You can cheat and buy ground (I sometimes do) but your curry will be not nearly as fragrant or fresh tasting. Like a bath with no bubbles. I used to be snobby about ground spices but, over time, I changed my mind. Buy spices in small quantities so they keep fresh. When you use spices you should be able to tell what it is just by smelling them i.e. mustard seed must smell like mustard.

Roasting spices is essential for releasing maximum flavour, good smells and nutritional benefits. Roast your spices slowly in a dry pan, separately from each other (if you can be bothered) as they toast at different rates. Be careful not to burn them as they will taste bitter and then your curry will too.

Grind them with a good old-fashioned pestle and mortar – or, less exciting and effective, a coffee grinder. The exception to this is turmeric, paprika and chili powder, which can only be bought ground, although if you want to grate your own turmeric you can buy the fresh root from Asian supermarkets, and you can make your own chilli powder by grinding chilies. Enjoy the process of grinding as a meditation and make sure to breathe in the intensely exotic, somewhat mystical aroma.

Chilli
(Miris)

A daring, energetic and exciting spice. Like most spices, it likes attention. Chilli, after all, is an aphrodisiac. Wear latex gloves when handling chilies or wash your hands thoroughly after use unless you want to burn your eyes! Alcohol or sugar will take the edge off the fiery heat if you have consumed too much.

There are over 400 varieties of chilli. On a rudimentary level, green chillies are the unripe version of their red or yellow cousins, which explains why the green variety are milder and slightly bitter in flavor. Green chillies are more commonly used in vegetable curries, while red chillies are used mainly for meat and fish curries.

Size matters when you are a chilli. The smaller the spicier. The seeds are the hottest bit so remove if you don't like too much heat. Dried chillies are sweeter and smokier in flavour. You can reduce their heat by soaking them in three parts mild wine vinegar to one part salt for one hour.

Chilli powder is a hot seasoning made from ground dried chillies, sometimes containing garlic, onion and other spices. Unroasted chilli powder is bright red in color whereas roasted chilli powder is dark browny red and adds a slightly smoky flavor. Chilli flakes are made from dried chillies that have been crushed whole, leaving flakes of the seeds.

Cinnamon
(Kurundu)

Proper cinnamon is lighter, thinner and more expensive than its rough sister Cassia. Sweet, warm and slightly bitter, it's a delicious natural sweetener and is native to Sri Lanka. It is truly lovely to seek out cinnamon quills being handmade on the South West Coast of Sri Lanka by skilfully peeling and rolling the bark. You will never mindlessly chuck a quill into a curry again.

Coriander seed, root & leaf
(Koththamalli)

Along with green chilli and lime, coriander is essential to every curry. The 'holy trinity' can lighten, cool, freshen and calm down saltiness, and cuts fattiness in a dish. Coriander seed, leaves and root are all used in Sri Lankan cooking. The dried and roasted beige seed is the main ingredient in curry powder (every Sri Lankan family has their own unique recipe) and is nutty, citrusy and warm tasting. It is an acquired taste, almost like toasted orange peel. Coriander root has a strong, intense flavour. The delicate leaves taste slightly of anise. Try to buy local from markets when you can, so you can get big, cheap bunches. Wash well as they can hold a lot of mud. The smell of coriander being washed is one of my favourite smells after the curry leaf frying in oil. Coriander leaves don't 'cook' well so add it last to your cooking.

Curry leaf
(Karapincha)

Curry leaves simmering in oil is a good smell. Native to India and Sri Lanka, they are picked from a tree and are often fried in oil with or without mustard seeds, which is known as 'tempering', before being used in curries, sambols and chutneys for an instant flavour hit. Curry leaves have a very distinctive, aromatic taste. Some people think you can substitute them with bay leaves or basil. I disagree. Never buy them in dried or powdered form; they are at their aromatic best when fresh. You can freeze the leaves but make sure they stay intact with the stems. There is a shortage of curry leaves in the UK and they are quite expensive, but you don't need very many to make a dish stand out and sing 'Sri Lanka'. In London, I buy them from Tooting Broadway, South Harrow or Brixton Village, but you can also buy them on Amazon.

Maldive fish
(Umbalakada)

An essential ingredient in Sri Lankan cooking, maldive fish is bonito tuna that has been boiled, smoked and then dried in the sun, which means it can keep without refrigeration. It is wonderful to see the fish drying along the streets on the south coast; a great flavour enhancer; a protein-rich thickening agent and umami hit. You can buy it from Asian supermarkets, or see the suggested subsitutes on page 23.

Pandan
(Rampé)

Most Sri Lankan households grow the pandanus plant, whose long green leaves are used to perfume curries and rice. Pandan is often referred to as the 'vanilla of Asia', such is its beautiful aroma. You can buy these in Chinatown or at asiancookshop.co.uk. I slice pandan into small pieces and freeze; they look like staples when frozen.

Tamarind
(Siyambala)

Rich fruit pulp found inside the tamarind seed pod, tamarind is sold as a pulp or puree concentrate from Asian supermarkets and online at Amazon and asiancookshop. co.uk (I like Por kwan brand). Like a sour date, it is tart and tangy and so used as a souring agent in a wide variety of meat and fish curries. Tamarind extract is actually found in good old friendly Worcester sauce, so it's therefore really nice with Sri Lankan cheese on toast (page 66) or swirl a dollop in yoghurt and serve with Sri Lankan shepherd's pie (page 84).

Turmeric
(Kaha)

A root like ginger but with a strong, woody flavour and a bright, warm yellowy-orangey-golden hue that adds colour to curries. It also has antiseptic, antioxidant and anti-inflammatory qualities – and stains permanently. Watch out! It can be bought whole in Asian supermarkets. Most Sri Lankan curries, if not all, will have a bit of turmeric.

2. Natural Sweeteners

Buffalo curd
(Mee kiri)

Not a natural sweetener, but buffalo curd is such a staple Sri Lankan ingredient and goes so well with treacle I decided to add it in here. Always what I crave after a fiery curry, or first thing in the morning. Similar to yoghurt made from buffalo milk naturally set and containing good-for-you probiotic cultures. People with dairy intolerances can even dig in, as it is not made from cow's milk.

Curd is sold in the most beautiful, charming clay pots in Sri Lanka. In the UK Laverstoke Park Farm do a range of organic buffalo products.

Jaggery
(Hakuru)

Unrefined palm sugar made by boiling palm tree sap and then pouring into coconut shells for a distinctive and characteristic shape, which can be grated or chopped into pieces. In powdered form it looks similar to brown sugar although it can vary in colour from light golden to dark brown and has a rich, caramel flavour. Always buy the darker, softer and crumblier jaggery.

Kithul treacle
(Kithul pani)

Made from the coconut or kithul palm. Kithul treacle is like a smokey maple syrup and my favourite natural sweetener. Make sure you buy stuff that is pure Kithul and doesn't have added sugar. Tastes very different region to region.

3. Fruit and Vegetables

There are many weird and wonderful wild and organic fruits and vegetables found in Sri Lanka. If you are lucky enough to find yourself out there then keep an eye out for some of these:

VEGETABLES:
Purple yams; rasavalli; moong bean; okra; lotus root; drumstick; bottle/bitter/ridge/snake gourd; capsicum; banana blossom; Gotu Kola (native pennywort); Manioc, jackfruit; 'white' sweet potato; ash pumpkin; taro; white radish; potato-like breadfruit; water spinach (known as kangknug) and long thin aubergines.

FRUIT:
Green-skinned narang; purple, plump lychee-tasting mangosteen; pink and spotted dragonfruit; sour, sweet Ambarella; the interesting 'cheese apple'; the many varieties of passionfruit; scarlet pomegranate; red and hairy rambutan; deep green soursop; and the controversial Woodapple.

My two most-used fruits that you might want to know more about are coconut and lime:

Coconut
(Pol)

Good-for-you coconut is the main ingredient in most Sri Lankan dishes. The husks and shell can also be used for anything from doormats and brooms to string and rope; the sap from the coconut tree can be used for making vinegar, treacle, plam sugar.

Coconut oil – *should be raw or extra virgin. It can be heated to higher temperatures than vegetable oil before it reaches smoking point – good to know.*
Coconut milk – *should always be full fat (you can thin it down with water if you want). I like the brand Chaokoh. A great flavour and low-sugar content.*
Coconut vinegar – *is made from the sap of the coconut tree or fermented coconut water. A good substitute would be rice vinegar.*
Raw, fresh coconut – *tastes milky, juicy and mild. When roasted it becomes more 'nutty' in flavor, like an almond.*
Orange 'king coconut' – *thambili are best for drinking.*

Lime
(Dehi)

Fresh lime juice is sold on every street in Sri Lanka, shaken with fresh cold water, salt and a bit of sugar. Limes are much bigger and juicier than the small, stubborn little tennis balls you get in the UK. A good tip is to roll the lime a couple of times to release the juices before slicing.

Then there are bananas, papayas, mangoes, pineapples, beetroot, courgette and all the other classics which are readily available in the UK and which I use in my recipes. However, they are much better tasting in Sri Lanka – worth a trip if only to taste the ripe and sunkissed produce!

Substituting ingredients

When I first started cooking Sri Lankan food I was adamant that it had to be as true to the original recipe as possible. As I've developed my style, I worry less about this, concentrating on how I can make use of what is readily available and how I can make it taste 'Sri Lankan'. It is unrealistic to always grate coconuts for sambol or make your own coconut milk – even if I might like to, it's not always convenient or accessible. My way of cooking is all about ease, balance, vibrancy, texture, colour and big-impact flavours.

I would love to have included recipes for all the amazing different vegetables you can find in Sri Lanka, for example breadfruit and fried bitter gourd. You will have to make an excuse to fly out to Sri Lanka yourself. Food is more special and memorable if you have to travel thousands of miles in order to taste it.

I encourage you to create lively dishes even if you don't have access to all the weird and wonderful produce out there, by using local produce or the substitutes listed opposite. I hope this book will inspire and excite your tastebuds.

I rate free-spirited, 'spontaneous' cooking. Seeing what I have in the fridge or at the market and going along with it creates wild 'off-piste' recipes. If you can't find one of the ingredients I've specified in the recipes that follow in a local supermarket or farmers' market, and you don't have time to wait for it to come online, here's what you can use instead:

EAST	WEST
PANDAN	*Buy fresh from Asian supermarkets and then strip widthways and freeze.*
JAGGERY	*Soft brown sugar or coconut sugar.*
FAT VANILLA PODS	*Good-quality vanilla extract*
MALDIVE FISH	*Oritz anchovies or fish sauce.*
KITHUL TREACLE	*Pure maple syrup.*
FRESH GOURDS	*Courgette, cucumber or celery.*
FRESH COCONUT MILK	*The best quality you can afford. I use Chaokoh brand bought on Amazon or powdered coconut.*
LEMONGRASS	*Buy fresh from Asian supermarkets then cut into small pieces and freeze. Susbtitute with fresh ginger and lemon juice.*
FRESH GRATED COCONUT	*Fresh frozen coconut or desiccated soaked in cold water. Cut into small pieces and freeze.*
CURRY LEAVES	*Buy fresh from Asian supermarkets – can be frozen.*
BUFFALO CURD	*Good quality full fat yoghurt – Total brand is great.*

1.

BREAKFAST

උදේ කෑම

Breakfast in Sri Lanka tends to be quite savoury, with curries and hoppers being just as popular early in the day as they are later on. I love having spice at breakfast as it wakes me up. Try it, you'll find it becomes addictive. Sri Lankans tend to have certain things solely dedicated to breakfast – milk rice, delicate string hoppers and kola kanda, for example – but you can have the recipes in this chapter any time of day. I particularly like breakfast food in the evenings, when you want something warm and comforting, like egg curry or dahl. You'll aslo find most of the recipes are gluten-free, as I use a lot of rice flour and oats, and dairy-free as I mainly use coconut milk or buffalo curd.

The hopper

ආප්ප

I have a real love for the humble hopper. Traditionally, egg and plain hoppers are served at breakfast or as a street-food snack in the towns of Sri Lanka. 'A hopper is a fermented pancake made with coconut milk and rice flour. It's nice!' was the slogan I used to chalk on a blackboard outside my hopper stall in Druid Street market. Like a crumpet, it's crispy on the outside and spongy and soft in the centre. It is sometimes made with an egg broken into the middle – by the time the hopper has cooked, the egg is perfectly poached in the little edible bowl.

The traditional method uses fresh toddy (pure alcohol derived from palm sap) in the batter instead of yeast for a natural fermentation. It isn't available in the UK, so I use dried yeast instead, which helps create the little 'crumpet' air holes.

There are lots of theories for achieving the perfect crunch, from adding egg whites to the batter to even using soaked marie biscuits. My secret ingredient is trisol, a soluble fibre derived from wheat. It's pretty expensive and not easy to find – I buy it online at Amazon – but if you are hopper serious, you should definitely invest in some. Your hopper is guaranteed to be of perfect crispiness and crunch if you do.

Once you have the recipe sorted, you can be as adventurous as you like with the fillings and could even add ground spices to the batter, or beetroot puree for an unconventional pink hopper; or swap the soda water for ginger beer/beer. I love the balancing act of the crispy hopper and the oozy egg, perhaps with Coconut sambol (page 154), roast peanuts and pungent mustard oil.

Tip – An egg can be used well past its sell-by date. To test if an egg is OK, place it in a bowl of cool water and if it sinks it fine – if it floats it's not.

Plain hopper

සරල ආප්ප

Serves 8–10

20g dried yeast

400ml coconut milk

1 tbsp caster sugar

300g red (or white) rice
flour, sifted

300g tapioca flour, sifted, or 100g
tapioca flour and 200g trisol

400ml coconut milk

1 tsp bicarbonate of soda, sifted

around 500ml fizzy water

1 egg per serving to make an
'egg' hopper (optional)

Whisk the yeast, coconut milk and caster sugar in a large bowl (the batter will rise!). Wrap with clingfilm and leave for 40 minutes in a warm place.

Add the flours (and trisol, if using), coconut milk, bicarbonate of soda and fizzy water to the consistency of double cream. Whisk and leave for a minimum of 2 hours (I usually leave overnight in a warm place unless in a hurry).

Once your hopper batter is bubbly and smells a bit like beer, it is ready. Heat a hopper pan or frying pan until it is hot but not smoking. Ladle about half a cup of batter into the pan and, once it starts to bubble, swivel a full 360-degree turn to coat the sides of the pan. Crack an egg into the middle of the pancake, if you like.

Cover the pan with a lid or tin foil and steam for 2–3 minutes until the sides of the hopper start to separate from the pan (and the egg is cooked, if using). With a wooden spatula, carefully remove the hopper and serve hot.

Every time you use the hopper mix, give it a good stir with a whisk as the batter will separate. You can freeze the mix freshly made, but if not the batter only lasts a day or so.

Ginger hopper & honey butter

ඉගුරු අප්ප සහ බටර් පැණි

Serves 8–10

500ml portion of basic hopper mix (see opposite)

4 tbsp ground ginger

6 tbsp brown sugar

½ tsp salt

For the honey butter:

75g salted butter, softened

65g honey

Play with the Egg Hopper:

Experimental fillings:

Duck egg

Double egg (Hopper Woppa)

English Breakfast Hopper with bacon, black pudding, roast tomatoes and mushrooms

Avocado, feta, Vegemite

White truffle, Parmesan

Marmite with plenty of butter

Chilli, crispy sage, prosciutto or anchovies

Seaweed, wasabi, cured trout

Variety of curries e.g. fried potato, pork

Experimental batters:

Apple puree

Beetroot puree

Turmeric powder

Lion lager batter

Ginger beer batter

Classic 'milk hoppers' are a national sweet favourite. This version tastes like a gingerbread man. The brown sugar activates the batter and makes it super-crisp and moreish.

First whip the butter with the honey and set aside. Whisk the ground ginger and brown sugar into the hopper mix and make the hopper following the directions above. Serve with the honey butter.

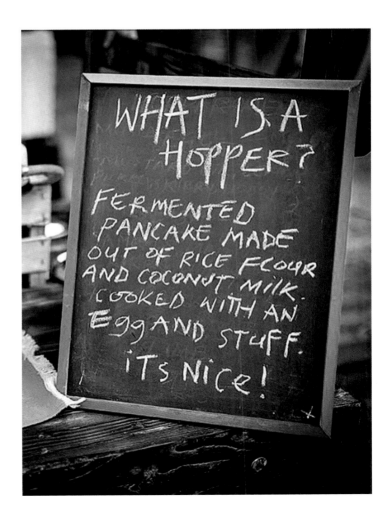

Sun House chilli eggs
හිරු නිවසක් මිරිස් බිත්තර

Serves 2

2 tbsp salted butter

120g shallots, peeled and
    finely chopped

1–2 small green chillies,
    finely chopped

230g finely chopped tomatoes

20g garlic, peeled and chopped

30g bunch coriander root, washed
    and finely chopped

4 medium free-range eggs

Parmesan cheese, as
    desired (optional)

2 anchovies, chopped (optional)

sea salt

freshly ground black pepper

To serve:

2 lime wedges

handful of coriander leaves

The Sun House in Galle – built in 1860 and owned by my eccentric uncle, Geoffrey Dobbs – was the original property that started the boutique hotel revolution in Sri Lanka. Lovely, attentive staff and full of character: battered, un-touristy and colonial. There's a room with an outside bath overlooking a view of palm trees, known as the 'Cinammon Suite'. We used to go at Christmas, bringing the turkey and Stilton from London and singing carols round the frangipani tree. The place hasn't changed in over 25 years.

These are notorious. Everybody loves The Sun House chilli eggs.

Heat a small non-stick frying plan (with a lid) and add half of the butter. When the butter is foaming add half of all the ingredients to the pan except the eggs, Parmesan and anchovies (if using). Stir and season with ¼ tsp salt and plenty of black pepper. Cook on a low heat for 4 minutes.

Carefully crack 2 of the eggs into the pan side by side and lightly season the yolks with a pinch of salt and pepper. Grate over the Parmesan and add anchovies on top if you want to make it more indulgent. Cover the pan and cook for 2–3 minutes until the whites of the eggs are set.

Repeat using the rest of the ingredients for the second serving.

Serve with a wedge of lime and coriander leaves sprinkled over the top.

Tip – If your pan doesn't have a lid, you can use tin foil instead – or a plate if you're desparate; just be careful when removing it as it will be hot.

Coconut and macadamia granola with kithul & red chilli

පොල් සහ මැකඩමියා කහ සමග

Makes I litre

(about 10 servings)

250g whole jumbo oats

140g rapeseed or groundnut oil,
      plus extra for greasing

1 tsp turmeric

½ tsp red chilli powder

2 tsp cinnamon powder

1 tsp ground ginger

zest of 2 limes

1 tsp sea salt

3 tbsp maple syrup or
      kithul treacle

80g macadamia nuts,
      roughly chopped

30g coconut chips

145g mixed tropical dried fruit
      (e.g. mango, pineapple),
      roughly chopped

To serve (optional):

handful of tropical fruit
      (e.g. passion fruit,
      mango, pineapple,
      papaya, pomegranate
      seeds) (optional)

coconut yoghurt or Buffalo
      curd labneh (page 37)

This granola is slightly salty, lightly spiced and a little sweet. You will be eating it straight from the jar. Highly addictive. It also makes a very good crunchy topping for a creamy oat porridge.

I use macadamias here, which are not Sri Lankan but their creamy, buttery richness and texture work so well with coconut. For the tropical dried fruit, Forest Feast – available at Waitrose and health food shops – do a great selection, including Slow-dried Cavendish Banana, Sour Mango and Coco Mango.

Preheat the oven to 150°C /fan 130°C/gas 2. Grease a 30 x 40cm baking tray and line with greaseproof paper.

In a large bowl, combine everything apart from the nuts, coconut chips and dried fruit with a large spoon. Transfer to the baking tray so you have an even layer and place in the oven for 25 minutes.

Take the mix out of the oven and stir. Cook for another 10 minutes, then add the nuts and coconut chips and gently mix. Return to the oven for 5 more minutes, then remove and spread the mixture out onto a clean, cool, wide baking tray in order to cool faster. Leave for 15 minutes then add the dried tropical fruit.

Serve with the toppings of your choice.

Buffalo curd labneh

Serves 4–6 as a side dish

1kg Laverstoke Park Farm
 buffalo milk yoghurt, or
 Total full-fat yoghurt

5–6cm piece fresh ginger,
 peeled and grated

zest of 2 limes

80g kithul treacle or maple syrup

1 tsp turmeric

pinch of saffron threads soaked in
 50ml hot water for 5 minutes

*To serve with sweet labneh
(optional):*

kithul treacle and fresh mango

Coconut and macadamia
 granola (page 36)

Coconut 'Scotch' pancakes
 (page 46)

Ceylon tea malt loaf (page 38)

Ginger hopper and honey
 butter (page 29)

Roast jackfruit (page 188)

*To serve with salted labneh
(optional):*

Tomato curry 'shakshuka'
 (page 40)

Pol roti (page 32)

Dhal (page 42)

Papaya radish, buffalo curd and
 chilli salad (page 145)

Wild mushrooms with chilli, arrack
 and yoghurt (page 152)

*The south of Sri Lanka is famous for buffalo curd, sold in
beautiful terracotta-colour clay pots. The curd is made from
fresh, unpasteurised buffalo milk, which is heated and then
cultured with a teaspoon of curd from the previous batch.*

*Utterly charming, particularly compared to western yoghurt
bought in plastic white tubs, buffalo curd is the real deal. Sri
Lankans don't alter their curd that much and commonly have
it just with smoky kithul treacle.*

*You will need a muslin cloth (available from most kitchen
shops and online). If you have any left over, try blending with
ice to make a drink or for salted labneh you can leave out the
kithul (and spices if you prefer), and add a little garlic and
salt.*

Combine all the ingredients in a bowl with a whisk. Transfer
to the centre of a clean muslin cloth and fold the edges over
the top. Place the muslin package in a sieve and rest on top
of a bowl for 1 hour in the fridge or a cool place, allowing the
flavours to develop and the yoghurt to firm and set as the
liquid filters to the bowl below. You want a luxurious yoghurt,
not a cheese, so an hour is enough. (If you leave overnight
you can whisk in a little milk to the labneh to achieve
whatever consistency you like.)

Serve with the toppings of your choice.

Ceylon tea malt loaf

ශ්‍රී ලංකා තේ ධාන්‍ය රොටියක්

Makes 1 loaf

165g malt extract, plus extra

115g jaggery or dark
        muscovado sugar

90ml coconut milk

1 tbsp ground cinnamon

1 tbsp ground ginger

45g tamarind paste

90g kithul treacle or maple syrup

1 tsp sea salt

200ml Ceylon loose-leaf tea,
        brewed for a minimum
        of 5 minutes

100g raisins

300g plain flour

2 tsp baking powder, sifted

To serve:

ghee or salted butter

Kaffir lime and lemongrass
        marmalade (page 220)

or Buffalo curd labneh (page 37)

In 1824 the British brought a tea plant from China to Ceylon. Soreen malt loaf is an old-school, British standard. This tea cake is a pimped-up Sri Lankan-style malt loaf. With a hard and robust crust on the outside and soft, sticky and squidgy on the inside. It's vegan-friendly too.

To make a cake ready to bake in 5 minutes, I use a 900g/2lb loaf tin and buy loaf tin liners made with non-stick siliconised paper, which you can get on Amazon. Cut slices thin and toast. Serve with lots of cold butter or ghee and kaffir lime and lemongrass marmalade.

Preheat the oven to 150°C/fan 130°C/gas 2 and line a loaf tin with 900g/2lb tin liners. Simples.

Combine the malt, sugar, coconut milk, cinnamon, ginger, tamarind paste, syrup and salt and stir in the hot tea (strained through a sieve) and raisins. Leave to soak for 10 minutes.

Tip in the flour, then quickly stir in the baking powder and pour into the loaf tin. Bake for 1 hour 10–15 minutes, depending on your oven, until firm. (It doesn't matter if it seems a little undercooked, it will firm up when cool.) While still warm, brush with a little more malt to glaze and leave to cool out of its tin. If you can hold out, it gets more sticky and squidgy after a few days and keeps for a week.

Tomato curry 'shakshuka'

තක්කාලි කරි

Serves 2–4

For the tomato curry:

700g vine-ripened tomatoes, (preferably datterini)

1 tbsp coconut oil or rapeseed oil

a handful of curry leaves

6cm piece pandan (optional)

1 cinnamon stick, broken

1 tsp fenugreek seeds

1 tbsp roasted curry powder (page 202)

1 tsp paprika

20g garlic, finely chopped

1 small red chilli, thinly sliced

20g fresh root ginger, peeled and finely grated

freshly ground black pepper

250g red onions, halved and finely sliced

130ml coconut milk

1 tsp jaggery or dark brown sugar

2–3 good-quality salted anchovies, roughly chopped

1 tbsp fish sauce

sea salt

To serve:

ghee

15g fresh coriander leaves

For the shakshuka:

4 eggs

5 anchovies (optional)

150g full-fat yoghurt

10g garlic, grated

1 tsp kithul or maple syrup

sea salt

Shakshuka is a middle eastern breakfast dish. Here I have made it Sri Lankan by using tomato curry rather than a spiced tomato sauce. Curries make wonderful leftovers and most freeze well. This is one such example: it is such a treat to have left-over tomato curry from the night before to whip up this impresive shakshuka. You could layer leftover Veena's aubergine curry (page 133) or Sweet potato curry (page 121) underneath the tomato curry if you want. Like Tunisians might add artichoke hearts or broad beans.

Slice the tomatoes in half and place in a large bowl. Heat the oil in a large frying pan or wok and, once about to smoke, add the curry leaves, pandan, cinnamon stick, fenugreek seeds, curry powder, paprika, garlic, chilli, ginger, black pepper and the onions with 1 tsp salt. Stir-fry for a couple of minutes then turn down the heat and sweat for 15 minutes or until the onions are really soft and sweet. If it begins to stick you can add a splash of water.

Add 100ml water and the coconut milk and simmer for 5 minutes. Finally, add the tomatoes, black pepper, jaggery or sugar, anchovies and fish sauce. Simmer for another 10 minutes until the tomatoes are just cooked, then leave to cool and check the seasoning. Serve with ghee stirred in at the end to thicken the curry and make it glossy, if you like, plus coriander leaves.

To make the 'shakshuka', pre-heat the oven to 180°C/fan 160°C/gas 4. Get a large, wide shallow pan, one that you don't mind bringing to the table and is suitable to go in the oven. Heat the curry until it's nice and hot, then drain a little of the liquid. Make four dents in the curry and gently crack the eggs into them. Season the yolks with a pinch of salt and black pepper. Scatter the anchovies over the top if you like. Cover the pan and place in the oven and cook for 10 minutes until the white is just set.

To serve:

lime wedges

Pol roti (page 32) or
    buttered toast

15g fresh coriander leaves

Smoked paprika/cayenne
    pepper (optional)

While the pan is in the oven, season the yoghurt with the grated garlic, syrup and a pinch of salt.

Remove the pan from the oven and serve immediately with the yoghurt, lime wedges, coriander leaves and warm Pol roti or lots of buttered toast to mop up the sauce. A sprinkle of smoked paprika or cayenne on top is nice too.

Dhal

ඇරිස්ස

Serves 4–6

350g red split lentils

2 green chillies

5cm pandan (if you have any)

½ garlic head, cut horizontally
    with skin on

1 tsp turmeric

1 cinnamon stick, broken in half

1 shallot, peeled

400ml coconut milk

2 tsp sea salt

175g spinach, washed

1 tsp chilli powder

For the temper:

1 tbsp coconut oil

1 tsp mustard seeds

handful of curry leaves

To serve (optional):

Pol roti (page 32)

Buffalo curd labneh (page
    37) or yoghurt

Crispy onions (page 203)

Dhal is a very popular breakfast dish in Sri Lanka – a bit like having a bowl of porridge. Tempering (heating spices in oil), gives a flavour booster. Leftover dhal watered down a little bit makes a warming and nourishing soup.

Pandan, or rampe, give off a warm citrus perfume and is used in sweet and savoury dishes. It can be added to most curries in this book if you are able to get hold of some. You can buy pandan in Southeast Asian shops or online at asiancookshop.com. You can't really substitute it so just leave it out if you don't have any. This keeps for a few days and freezes well.

Soak the lentils in cold water while you get together the rest of your ingredients.

Drain the lentils and transfer to a large pan with 800ml water, the whole green chillies, pandan, garlic, turmeric, cinnamon and shallot and simmer on a low heat, uncovered, for 10 minutes. Add the coconut milk to the pan and cook for 15 minutes or until the lentils are soft. Then add the salt (you add it at the end as doing so beforehand prevents the lentils from cooking).

Once the lentils are cooked, turn off the heat and fish out the pandan, garlic and shallot with tongs and discard. Add the spinach and chilli powder to the lentils.

To make the temper, heat the oil in a small pan. Once it starts to smoke add the mustard seeds, quickly followed by the curry leaves. Pour into the dhal and serve with toppings and sides of your choice.

Milk rice

කිරි බත්

Serves 2–4

200g glutinous (sticky) rice

1 tsp salt

4 green cardamom pods, bruised

100ml coconut milk

2 tbsp kithul treacle or rice syrup

To serve (optional):

Lunumiris (page 32) or

banana and brown sugar or

Kaffir lime and lemongrass
    marmalade (page 220),
    warmed through with
    a splash of water

Milk rice (kiri bath) is eaten at breakfast on the first day of each month and on special occasions, and is traditionally shaped like a diamond. It has been part of Sri Lanka's culinary heritage for 2,500 years. Made with glutinous rice, this thick rice pudding is extra sticky and sweet. Make it fresh and eat the same day – it does not freeze.

Soak the rice in cold water while you boil the kettle. Drain the rice, then put it in a pan (with a lid) with the salt, cardamoms and 300ml boiled water. Stir to ensure the rice hasn't stuck to the bottom, then cover and cook on a low heat for 10 minutes. If it starts to smoke the pan is too hot so turn down the heat. Take the pan off the heat for 10 minutes and allow to steam in the residual heat with the lid on.

Combine the coconut milk and syrup and add to the rice. Once absorbed, gently pour the rice onto a small 21 x 17 cm baking tray and put in the fridge or a cool place for 10 minutes or so. Once cool, cut into diamonds. Eat hot or cold with toppings of your choice.

Kola kanda

කොළ කැඳ

Serves 4

75g red rice
800ml water
¼ tsp sea salt
400ml coconut milk
25g parsley, chopped
25g coriander, chopped
15g mint, chopped
zest of 1 lime
50g spinach, washed

To serve:
crumbled jaggery or
    brown sugar
freshly shaved coconut
    (optional)

A sort of a warm savoury rice smoothie, Kola kanda in Sri Lanka is made with Ayurvedic gotu kola – similar to pennywort – one of the island's most widely available leafy greens. Its leaves bear some resemblance to the shape of the human brain, and it is said to bring enlightenment and longevity. Unfortunately, this ancient herb isn't easily available in the UK so I use a mix of fresh herbs instead. You can find red rice in Asian supermarkets or online at the Asian cookshop. Alternatively you could replace it with any kind of rice you want, or I sometimes use spelt.

Soak the rice in cold water while you collect together the rest of your ingredients.

Boil the water in a heavy-based saucepan. Drain the rice and add to the pan with the salt. Simmer, uncovered, over a medium heat for 20–25 minutes until the rice has broken up and the soup is thick.

Meanwhile, blend the coconut milk with the herbs, lime zest and spinach. Once the rice is cooked and the water has mostly evaporated, remove from the heat and stir the herby coconut milk into the mix. Serve warm in tall glasses with crumbled jaggery or brown sugar and freshly shaved coconut, if you like.

Coconut 'Scotch' pancakes

ඇණවුම් පොල්-කසෙලේ පෑන්කෙ'ක්

Serves 4

2 large ripe bananas

2 medium free-range eggs

100g white or red rice flour

1 tsp ground cinnamon
    or cardamom

100ml coconut milk

½ tsp sea salt

½ tsp bicarbonate of soda, sifted

100g desiccated or freshly
grated coconut

1 tsp coconut oil (optional)

To serve:

full-fat yoghurt, buffalo curd
    or ghee as desired

maple syrup or kithul treacle

2 limes, cut into wedges

4 bananas, sliced

These remind me of the old-fashioned Scotch pancakes my mum used to buy in packets, but these are dairy-, sugar- and gluten-free. You will need a non-stick frying pan that does what it says.

Preheat the oven to 180°C/fan 160°C/gas 4.

In a bowl, mash up the bananas and eggs with a whisk or fork. Add the rice flour, cinnamon, coconut milk, salt and bicarbonate of soda and combine until it all forms a nice batter. Don't worry about a few banana lumps.

Once the oven is hot, toast the desiccated coconut on a baking tray for 3 minutes. Leave to cool. Then add half of the toasted coconut to the mix.

Grease your non-stick frying pan with coconut oil if it's a bit unreliable. Place the pan over a low heat and add about 2–3 tablespoons of the mixture to the pan for each pancake (Scotch pancake-sized). Shake the pan slightly so that the batter evens out.

Once bubbles start to form (after about 1 ½ minutes) flip and cook on the other side.

Serve with the yoghurt, a scattering of the remaining toasted coconut, maple syrup or kithul treacle, lime wedges and fresh banana slices.

Tip – You could replace the bananas with 85g full-fat yoghurt or buffalo curd, along with 2 tablespoons of maple syrup, and use fresh coconut instead of toasted.

String hoppers

ඉදි අප්ප

Serves 6–8 as a side

You will need:
hopper mould
2-4 bamboo mats
steamer

500g red rice flour
1 tsp sea salt

To serve:
Egg curry (page 34) and/
   or dhal (page 42)
sambol of your choice
   (pages 154–157)

String hoppers are steamed rice noodles eaten at breakfast with egg curry and/or dhal. Light, fluffy and delicately lacy, something cool happens when they are fried (see page 64).

Apart from needing a hopper mould and bamboo mats, string hoppers are easy to make – and a recipe you can get kids involved in (the dough is a bit like Play-Doh). If you don't have the time or the gear, though, then you can buy them pre-made from Asian supermarkets or replace with rice vermicelli. String hoppers also make a good alternative to pasta.

First prepare a saucepan with enough water so it doesn't touch the base of the steamer.

In a large bowl, combine the flour and salt with 500ml warm water and use your hands to mix until a soft dough forms – a little bit softer than playdough. The consistency is very important – too wet or too dry will ruin your string hoppers. Don't worry if it takes a couple of attempts before you get it right – it's quite fun.

Place a small amount of the dough on a dry string hopper mould (the dough will stick if it is wet) and squeeze out onto the bamboo mats, starting in the centre then working outwards (as shown opposite). Stack the mats on top of each other and steam for 4 minutes. Serve with the dhal, egg curry and sambol.

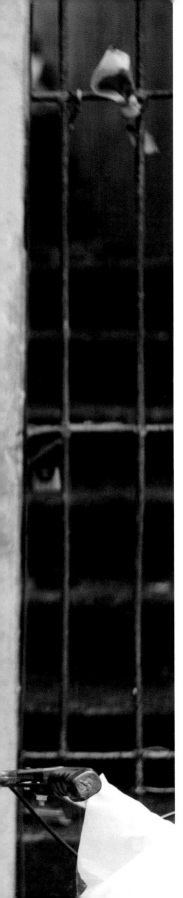

2.
SHORT EATS

සුළු කැම

Sri Lankans are big eaters, so savoury, salty and spicy snacks known as short eats are very popular over there and are eaten any time of day. There are hundreds of kiosks, roadside stalls, bread vans, pots boiling with sweetcorn husks and street vendors around the country, including on trains and buses – solely dedicated to selling short eats such as super-cheap vadai, peanuts, cutlets and mutton rolls.

Most of these short eats would make a good starter, snack, canapé or side dish – or a main course if you wanted something light and easy. Always eat them with your hands rather than with a fork. Curries are also eaten this way – always with the right hand if you want to stick to Sri Lankan tradition.

Tuna and avocado cutlets with cucumber pickle

පිපිඤ්ඤා අච්චාරු සමග ටූනා හා අලිගැට පේර අසල සිටි

Serves 6–8

450g fresh tuna, roughly
    chopped into small chunks

80g shallots, finely chopped

1 small avocado, chopped

handful of coriander stalk,
    finely chopped

2 spring onions, white part
    only, finely chopped

2 tsp Roasted curry
    powder (page 202)

40g fine breadcrumbs

1 tsp black pepper

1½ tsp sea salt

juice of ½ lime

2 small green chillies,
    finely chopped

20g fresh ginger, peeled
    and finely chopped

15g garlic, peeled and
    finely choppped

9 spring roll wrappers

1 egg

300g fine breadcrumbs

To serve:
Cucumber pickle (page 213)

Lime and coriander yoghurt
    sauce (page 209)

Lunumiris (page 32)

2 limes, cut into wedges

handful of coriander
    or dill leaves

Sri Lanka's croquette, cutlets are a cult street-food snack. Sahana, off the main street in Galle, do very good ones as do the stalls by the town's train station. Out there, cutlets are deep-fried, spicy and breaded and made with minced meat or fish and potatoes. This recipe is less heavy, as they are baked instead of fried (there is no potato) and the binding ingredient is avocado, resulting in a juicy, moist fish cutlet. I like to serve them warm with a sharp, tangy cucumber pickle to lift and freshen, plus extra avocado, fresh herbs and baby gem lettuce.

Preheat the oven to 240°C/fan 220°C/gas 9 and line a baking tray with baking paper.

Place all your ingredients in a blender except the spring roll wrappers, egg and second lot of breadcrumbs (300g). Combine until you have a rough paste. Divide the mix evenly into 24 pieces and use your hands to roll them into balls (a little smaller than a golf ball).

Soak each spring roll wrapper in warm water for 10 seconds, then cut in half. Roll each ball in a wrapper, cutting off the excess to save it for the next ball. This will make your ball easier to manage and extra crispy. They will keep nicely like this for a day or so in the fridge if you want to make in advance.

When you are ready to cook, lightly beat the egg in one bowl and place the remaining breadcrumbs in a separate bowl. Roll each ball in the egg then the breadcrumbs.

Transfer the balls to the baking tray and bake for 10–12 minutes on the top shelf of the oven. The cutlets should be golden brown on the outside and just cooked. Leave to cool slightly and then serve with cucumber pickle, coriander yoghurt sauce or coconut oil mayo with a swirl of lunumiris, lime wedges and coriander or dill leaves.

Brown shrimp vadai with cashew nut dipping sauce

කජු කරන්නා වූ පෑෂ්ඨී වෙනස්කිරීමේ

Serves 4

200g dry yellow split peas,
    soaked overnight
    in cold water

400g tinned chickpeas

50g spring onions

25g coriander stalk

15g ginger

15g garlic

½ tsp chilli powder

1 tsp turmeric

2 tsp sea salt

1 egg

80g breadcrumbs

juice of 2 large limes

½ tsp baking soda, sifted

180g brown shrimps

For the dipping sauce:

70g cashew nuts

10g garlic, peeled and
    roughly chopped

10g fresh ginger, peeled and
    roughly chopped

200ml groundnut oil

1 tsp sea salt

½ tsp turmeric

juice of 1 lime

1 tbsp kithul treacle or
    maple syrup

To serve:

2 limes, cut into wedges

handful of coriander leaves

Along Colombo's Galle Face Green, there are children flying kites, deep red hazy sunsets and romantics holding hands. The promenade by the Indian Ocean and its crashing waves hosts lots of little racing-green kiosks selling crispy, deep-fried patties with whole prawns known as isso vadai – pronounced vad-ay – Sri Lanka's version of falafels. You can also find them on trains on the way up to Kandy or from Ella.

These vadai are slightly lighter as they are baked instead of fried. I add brown shrimp to give them a bit of Englishness.

Preheat the oven to 200°C/fan 180°C/gas 6 and line a baking tray with baking paper.

Drain the split peas in a colander with the chickpeas. Roughly chop the spring onions, then blend with the coriander, ginger and garlic to a paste in a food processor and then add everything else except for the brown shrimps. Blend until well combined.

Take out of the blender and then place in a large bowl and mix in the brown shrimps. Roll into little balls the size of a golf ball and transfer to the baking tray. Bake in the oven for 20–30 minutes, depending on how big your vadai are. They should be brown and crispy.

For the cashew nut dipping sauce, roast the cashews in the oven at 180°C/fan 160°C/gas 4 for 5 minutes and allow to cool. Then whizz with all the other ingredients in a blender until smooth. Serve with the shrimp vadai, lime wedges and coriander leaves.

Deep-fried whitebait

ගැඹුරු තෙලෙන් බැදපු මාථ

Serves 4–6

vegetable oil, for deep-frying

250g whitebait or fresh
anchovies

1 tsp sea salt

1 tsp freshly ground
black pepper

1 tsp cayenne pepper

1 tsp turmeric

2 tsp lime juice

140g rice flour

To serve:
plenty of Coconut oil and
lime mayo (page 206)

I love the medieval-style kitchens you find in Sri Lanka – open fires, palm-woven ceilings, old copper pans and clay pots. Like you have stepped back in time. Galipita Rocks is an eco-lodge with a medieval kitchen surrounded by cascading waterfalls and a moody lake. At night you can see the Milky Way while lying on the huge rocks still warm from the sun. The perfect setting for a snack of deep-fried whitebait.

In a wok or large saucepan, heat enough vegetable oil to achieve a 5cm depth. Bring the temperature of the oil up to 170°C/340F – use a kitchen thermometer to check.

Meanwhile, wash the whitebait. Dry with kitchen paper then put in a bowl with the rest of the ingredients except the flour and toss to mix. Spread the flour on a large plate and lay the fish in the flour and roll around to cover. Get rid of any excess flour by putting the whitebait in a clean sieve and shaking gently.

Fry the fish in the hot oil in batches so as not to overcrowd the pan, for a couple of minutes each until nice and crisp. Remove with a slotted spoon and spread out on a baking tray lined with baking paper to blot the grease. Serve immediately with lots of coconut oil mayo.

Clams in rum, tamarind butter and cinnamon with string hoppers

ඉඳියාප්ප සමග රම්, සියඹ ලා බටර් සහ

Serves 4

1kg palourde clams

string hoppers (shop-bought or page 26) or rice vermicelli

85g tamarind butter (page 218) or 85g salted butter or ghee with 1 tbsp tamarind paste

10g garlic, peeled and finely chopped

10g fresh ginger

2 small red chillies, chopped

handful of curry leaves (if possible)

1 cinnamon stick, broken in half

3 tsp brown sugar or jaggery

85ml dark rum

To serve:
Pol roti (page 32)

You can't get clams or mussels in Sri Lanka, but if you could I would like to have this in the afternoon at monsoon, when it is dark, stormy and atmospheric. Serve with fresh warm roti if you like. You could use the same method for mussels, razor clams or cod cheeks.

Discard any clams with broken shells or that do not shut when tapped. Scrub with a scourer to remove any barnacles and keep in an empty bowl (not in water) covered with a damp cloth.

Boil the kettle and soak the string hoppers or vermicelli for a couple of minutes and then drain and stir so they don't stick.

Heat a large heavy-based saucepan (with a lid) and add the tamarind butter with the garlic, ginger, chillies, curry leaves, cinnamon and sugar. Fry for a couple of minutes then deglaze with the dark rum. Add the clams and immediately put on a tight-fitting lid. Cook for 5 minutes on a high heat until all the clams have opened and the rum is cooked. (Discard any clams that refuse to open.) Stir in the soaked string hoppers or vermicelli and finish with the lime juice and coriander leaves.

Mussels, lime & chilli butter in arrack

අරක්කු ගැන අරක්කු, දෙහි හා මිරිස්

Serves 4

1kg mussels

2 tbsp coconut oil

10g garlic, peeled and
    thinly sliced

1 large shallot, peeled
    and thinly sliced

20g coriander stalk,
    finely chopped

handful of curry leaves
    (if possible)

250ml arrack

3 tsp kithul treacle or
    maple syrup

½ tsp turmeric

1 tbsp chilli butter (page 218)

juice of 1 lime

pinch of sea salt

handful of coriander leaves

To serve:
Pol roti (page 32)

Not native to Sri Lanka however super-cheap, quick and easy to make. Buy your mussels live and shut tight from your local fishmonger. Store before use in a cool, damp place – the sink. This way you can clean them, by removing the barnacles and beards, in a self-contained, no-mess cool box.

Rinse the mussels under cold water, removing the beards by pulling them sharply towards you. Discard the shells that don't close when tapped with a knife.

Heat the coconut oil in a large pan (with a lid). Once hot, add the garlic, shallot, coriander stalk and curry leaves and sizzle for a couple of minutes. Add the mussels, give the pan a good shake and cook for a minute. Add the arrack, treacle or syrup and turmeric and then immediately cover the pan with a lid and let it steam.

Cook for 5 minutes, giving the pan a good shake. Check the mussels have opened and add the chilli butter to emulsify the liquid, add the lime juice and salt, and finish with the chopped coriander. Discard any shells that haven't opened.

Serve the mussels with fresh pol roti.

Mutton rolls

එළු මස් රෝ ි

Serves 2–4

270g sweet potatoes

3 tbsp vegetable oil

270g lamb mince

2 tsp sea salt

2 tsp freshly ground
    black pepper

2 tbsp malt vinegar

85g red onion, finely chopped

1 or 2 small green chillies,
    finely chopped

15g fresh ginger, peeled
    and finely chopped

15g garlic, peeled and
    finely sliced

1 tsp brown sugar

1 tsp ground cinnamon

1 tbsp Maldive fish flakes or
    3 anchovies, chopped

handful of mint leaves,
    finely chopped

handful of parsley,
    finely chopped

50g breadcrumbs

For the coating:

3 large spring roll wrappers

1 egg, lightly beaten

165g fine breadcrumbs

To serve:

Cucumber or Pineapple
    pickle (page 213)

Coriander chutney (page 109)

Mutton rolls are considered a staple food in Sri Lanka; you can buy them ready-made in street cadays and from vendors all over the country.

Here I have used minced lamb rather than mutton as it is more easily available, and sweet potato as I love the combination of the two. You could mince leftover lamb curry and use that instead, or make the mix a day or so before you roll to save you time.

Preheat the oven to 180°C/fan 160°C/gas 4. Wrap each of your sweet potatoes in tin foil and roast for 1 hour. Meanwhile, prep and measure out the rest of your ingredients.

Heat the oil in a large saucepan and, once it begins to smoke, add the lamb and salt and pepper. Brown the meat, breaking it up with a wooden spoon. Add the vinegar and allow the liquid to evaporate in the hot pan (about 8 minutes).

Add the onions, green chillies, ginger, garlic, sugar and cinnamon. Bash the maldive fish flakes in a pestle and mortar, if using, and add these or the anchovies to the pan too. Cook, stirring continuously, for 5 minutes. Take off the heat and stir in the mint, parsley and breadcrumbs. Stir until well mixed and leave to one side until the sweet potato is ready.

When the sweet potatoes are cooked, remove from the oven, turning it up to 200°C /fan 180°C/gas 6. Carefully peel while warm. Add to the meat mixture in the pan and stir until well combined. Leave to cool for a few minutes and season with ½ tsp sea salt.

Soak the spring roll wrapper in warm water for about 10 seconds then stretch and lay out on a plate. Put the lamb and potato mix down the centre of each wrapper in a long line like you are wrapping up a spring roll. Cut each in half and then roll in egg then breadcrumbs. Make about 6 rolls.

Place on the baking tray lined with baking paper and bake for about 30 minutes until golden and crisp, turning each over halfway.

Remove from the oven and leave to cool slightly, before serving warm with pickles and/or Coriander chutney.

Deep-fried string hoppers with crab mayo

ගැඹුරු තෙලෙන් බැදූ ඉදි අප්ප සමග කකුළු මස්

Serves 4–6

5 ready-made string
   hoppers, shop-bought
   or see page 26
50ml vegetable oil, for
   deep-frying

For the crab mayonnaise:
150g picked white crabmeat
75g Coconut oil and lime
   mayo (page 206)
lime juice and sea salt, to taste
4 spring onions, thinly sliced
handful of torn basil leaves,
   plus extra to finish

I made these as snacks at Colombo Fashion Week 2016 and they were an instant hit. Sweet, juicy crab in little crunchy nests.

Gently break the lacy string hoppers in half prior to cooking for canapés, or keep whole if you want to serve as a starter. This works OK(ish) with rice vermicelli noodle nests too, but it's best with string hoppers as they are the right size and crunch.

First, make the crab mayonnaise. Stir the crab into the coconut oil mayonnaise with a fork and add the lime juice and salt. You might want to add more lime juice and a pinch of salt. Add the spring onions and basil leaves and stir through. Set aside in the fridge.

You can bake the string hoppers in the oven at 180°C/fan 160°C/gas 4 for 10 minutes if you prefer, but something magical happens when you deep-fry them. They sort of explode and pop and go extra crisp. Get a wide saucepan and heat the oil. If you're making canapés, carefully break the string hoppers in half, otherwise leave whole.

Once the oil is very hot, add about 4 string hopper baskets and fry for a couple of minutes, then turn over with some tongs or a slotted spoon and fry the other side. Drain on kitchen paper.

Immediately dollop a tablespoon of crab mayonnaise onto each portion while the string hoppers are warm and sprinkle with basil leaves.

Sri Lankan cheese on toast

ශ්‍රී ලංකන් චීස් සමග ටෝ ,

Serves 2

butter or ghee

2 slice bread (whatever kind
you like), toasted

2 tbsp date and tamarind
jam, store-bought
mango chutney or, even
better, leftover Fried
leeks (page 162)

2 juicy ripe tomatoes, sliced

170g mature Cheddar and/
or Gruyère, grated

2 medium free-range
egg, whisked

1 tsp mustard powder

1 tsp turmeric

1 tsp chilli powder

1 tsp tamarind paste

freshly ground black
pepper, to taste

½ tsp sea salt

3 spring onion, thinly sliced

To serve:
lime wedges

a few coriander leaves

Fried leeks (page 162 –
optional)

Cucumber pickle (page
213 – optional)

Tamarind and date chutney
(page 218 – optional)

*Tamarind is used a lot in Sri Lanka and I love to cook with it.
I use it so often I now buy it as a paste rather than extracting it
from the seedy pulp. Por Kwan brand is good; you can find it at
Waitrose or online at Amazon.*

*This is based on Britain's classic cheese on toast, but with
tamarind instead of Worcestershire sauce (which actually has
tamarind extract in it). You can play with what you like inside
but a dollop of leftover Fried leeks or chard is the dream, as is
Cucumber pickle.*

Preheat the grill to hot.

Butter the toast and spread each with a tablespoon of
tamarind jam followed by the sliced tomato seasoned with
a little salt. Set aside – it doesn't matter if your toast gets a
little cold.

Combine the rest of the ingredients in a bowl and then spread
evenly onto each tomato toast. Place under the hot grill for 5
minutes or until bubbling. You want it crisp on top and melted
all the way through.

Serve with lime wedges and the coriander leaves, plus Fried
leeks, Cucumber pickle or Tamarind and date chutney, if you
like.

Curry buns

 මාළු පාන්

Makes 8–9 curry buns

80ml coconut milk

1 tsp sea salt

2 tsp sugar

45g butter, plus extra
   for greasing

15g dried yeast

450g white spelt flour, plus
   extra for dusting

500g leftover curry – Black
   pork (page 85), Venison
   (page 82) or Sweet
   potato (page 121)

1 egg yolk, beaten

To serve:
Salted buffalo curd
   labneh (page 37)

Tamarind and date chutney
   (page 218)

Curry buns remind me of the loud tune of 'Für Elise' playing from the south coast's little bread vans. The cult breakfast bun can be eaten any time of day and you can pretty much fill with any type of curry – fish buns are very popular, and a Sweet potato curry bun would work well too, but the slightly sweet bun and the juicy Black pork curry is a real winner.

Put the coconut milk into a saucepan and bring to the boil. Remove from the heat and stir in the salt, sugar and butter and allow to cool to lukewarm.

Put the yeast in a bowl, pour over 200ml cold water and stir until dissolved. Add the lukewarm milk mixture and leave for 40 minutes in a warm place, covered with a tea towel, to rise slightly.

Come back to the mixture and sift in the flour. Mix together, then knead with your hands in the bowl until smooth, adding just enough of the extra flour to make a soft dough.

Turn the dough out onto a lightly floured surface and knead for about 10 minutes until smooth and elastic, adding a little more flour if you find it sticking to a surface.
Shape into a ball and place in a greased bowl (to prevent the dough from sticking to it). Cover with a clean tea towel and set aside in a warm place for about an hour or until it has doubled in size.

Preheat the oven to 200°C/fan 180°C/gas 6 and line two baking trays with greaseproof paper.

cont.

When the hour is almost up/the dough has nearly doubled in size, warm the curry through with a splash of water. If using venison or pig's cheek, shred the meat so it's nice and juicy and soft and then leave to cool. Once the dough is ready, divide the dough into 8–9 golf ball-sized pieces and flatten each portion into a circle. Place a spoonful of the cooled curry in the centre. Bring the edges of the dough together, pressing and moulding to seal the curry inside.

Arrange the buns, seam side down, on the baking trays, allowing enough space for rising and spreading, about 4cm between each one. Cover with a clean tea towel and leave in a warm place for 30 minutes until nearly doubled in size.

Brush the top of each bun with the beaten egg yolk to glaze, and bake for 20 minutes or until golden brown. Leave to cool for a few minutes if you can resist, and serve the buns on their own or with date and tamarind jam. These don't keep well and are best eaten within 3 hours of cooking.

3.
CURRY

ව්‍යංජන

I hope this chapter will help you feel less intimidated about cooking curry and lose the idea that it has to be rich, overly spicy, or drowning in sauce, when actually it can be quick to make, light and fresh. Curries are perfect for sharing and most freeze easily and make wonderful leftover dishes.

Sri Lankans often separate their curries by the level of spice. A 'white' curry is mild, 'red' is moderate and a 'black' curry is not for the faint-hearted. The traditional method is to cook the curry on open fire in clay pots. I love this medieval idea. The open flames also help to give a smoky, deep flavour.

Sri Lankan eating is sort of like mezze, large sharing plates with a mixture of fish, meat and vegetarian dishes, salads and rice. These curries are designed to be eaten together rather than on their own. I like to serve my curries with a little less rice than traditional with plenty of fresh green salad, fried poppadum, sweet chutneys and sour pickles. Two people should share a minimum of three curries and a salad, four people about six.

Rather than buying ready-made 'curry pastes' it is so easy to make a curry from scratch. Once you know how, you can pretty much curry anything you want. The curry bases (pages 78 and 114) should help you do your own thing and explore coming up with your own curries. Always taste as you go and don't be afraid to experiment a bit. Sri Lankans don't tend to weigh ingredients, they judge by sight and taste instead.

Top tip from me: to make clearing up easier, I get a large bowl when I'm prepping all my ingredients and use it as a dustbin. All my onion, garlic skins, okra ends etc. go into that and it makes the whole process much easier. Adopt this method every time you cook. You want to prep all your ingredients ready to go before you start a recipe so you can work quickly and efficiently. It will only make life easier for yourself.

3.1
MEAT

ම ස්

Basic meat curry

මූලික මස් කරි

Serves 4–6

1 tbsp vegetable or coconut oil

handful of curry leaves

1 tsp black mustard seeds

1 tsp cumin seeds

1 red onion, finely sliced

1 tsp sea salt

20g garlic, peeled and finely sliced

20g fresh ginger, peeled and
finely chopped

2–3 green or red chillies, deseeded and finely chopped

1 lemongrass stalk, bruised
(optional)

1 small bunch coriander,
stalks only, finely
chopped (optional)

1 cinnamon stick, broken in half

1 tbsp jaggery or brown sugar

200ml coconut milk

100ml water

200g tinned chopped
tomatoes (optional)

Choice of meat:

500g beef, chicken, lamb,
pork, roughly cut into
4–5cm chunks

vegetable, groundnut or
coconut oil

*Choice of spices (choose 3–4 on
top of curry powder):*

1 tbsp roasted curry
powder (page 202)

1 tsp turmeric

1 tsp toasted fenugreek

4 cloves

4 cardamom pods

1 tsp chilli powder

This is your blank canvas, so to speak. A meat curry base you can use as your starting point to get experimenting with your own ideas. You'll find it's pretty much the same as the vegetable base on page 114, but I slow-cook the onions for a long time so they're extra sweet and soft. I also like to brown and slow-cook meat when making curry. This way you get soft, rich and juicy pieces full of character and depth rather than chewy and tough.

Fish and meat like ginger and lemongrass, whereas vegetables are less bothered. A cinnamon stick or two is mandatory in every Sri Lankan curry.

First prep your ingredients so everything is organised and good to go, and preheat the oven to 160°C/fan 140°C/gas 3.

Heat the oil in a large heavy-based saucepan (with a lid). Just before it starts to smoke, add the curry leaves, followed by the mustard seeds and cumin seeds. The mustard should crackle and pop immediately. Turn down the heat (otherwise your mustard seeds will burn and become bitter) and quickly add the onion. Season with the salt. Slow-cook until the onions are really soft – about 30 minutes.

While this is going on, prep and brown your meat. In a separate large pan heat a good amount of oil. When just about to smoke, add the meat, making sure there is enough room in the pan so it browns and doesn't steam-cook. Cook in batches if you have to and set aside.

Add the garlic, ginger, chillies and, if using, the lemongrass and coriander stalks to the pan with the softened onion. Allow to cook for 2 minutes then add the cinnamon stick and spices of your choice along with the jaggery or brown sugar. Cook for 2 minutes then add the browned meat and stir so everything is nicely coated in the oil, spices and garlic mix.

To serve:

juice of 1 lime

handful of coriander leaves

Then add the coconut milk, water and chopped tomatoes, if using. Simmer for a couple of minutes, then cover and cook in the oven for 3–4 hours.

Serve with a squeeze of lime juice and a scattering of coriander leaves.

Chicken liver curry

කුකුළු අක්මා කරි

Serves 2–4 as a side

400g chicken livers, chopped
        into 4cm chunks

1 tbsp roasted curry
        powder (page 202)

2 tbsp ground nut or rapeseed oil

1 tsp cumin seeds

½ red onion, finely chopped

2 green chilli, de-seeded,
        finely chopped

15g garlic, finely chopped

1 tsp sea salt

½ tsp turmeric

1 tsp freshly ground black pepper

25g salted butter (tamarind is
        good if you have any spare)

½ lime, juice

handful of pomegranate jewels

coriander or mint leaves

To serve:

Crispy onions or Crushed
        poppadom (both page
        203 – optional)

Creamy chicken liver, crispy skin and bursts of juicy pomegranate. Not only do they have a deeper richer flavour to other parts of the bird, they are fast to cook, cheaper and ethical. To cook just right (crispy on the outside and slightly pink on the inside) you will need a very hot wide pan. This can be made in advance and can also be frozen.

Place the chunks of chicken liver in a bowl with the curry powder to marinate and set aside.

Heat the oil in a wide hot pan and when it is just about to smoke add the cumin seeds followed by the onion, chilli, garlic and salt. Cook for 5 minutes, then add the turmeric.

Carefully add the chicken livers in batches so as not to overcrowd the pan, along with the pepper. Cook on one side for 3 minutes in a very hot pan then, when brown, cook on the other side.

Quickly add the butter, lime juice and 100ml water to deglaze the pan and then place the livers in a separate bowl with the pomegrante jewels and coriander leaves. The chicken livers should be tender and juicy. Serve with Crispy onions and Crushed poppadom for added texture and colour, if you like.

Venison curry

මුව මස් ව්‍යංජන

Serves 4

1kg venison haunch (or you
    can use lamb's neck),
    cut into 3cm chunks

265g unripe green papaya
    flesh (optional)

2 tbsp freshly ground
    black pepper

5 tbsp coconut or vegetable oil

10 curry leaves (if possible)

4 red onions, peeled and sliced

10cm pandan leaf, chopped into
    2cm pieces (if you can find)

15g garlic, peeled and
    finely chopped

15g fresh ginger, peeled and
    finely chopped

25g coriander root, washed
    and finely chopped

3–4 small green chillies,
    finely chopped

4 Ortiz anchovies, chopped, or 2
    tbsp fish sauce (optional)

2 tbsp roasted curry
    powder (page 202)

2 tsp turmeric

2 cinnamon stick, broken in half

400ml coconut milk

2 tbsp coconut vinegar
    or rice vinegar

300ml water

1 tbsp brown sugar or jaggery

200g cherry tomatoes, halved

1 tbsp full-fat yoghurt (optional)

sea salt and freshly ground
    black pepper

Meat in Asia is not always premium quality; it isn't hung and more often than not is extremely tough. Therefore, papaya is said to act as a tenderiser. I'm not sure it makes a difference but I think the idea is cool. Slow-cooking ensures the meat in this curry will be succulent and juicy so don't worry.

Venison (or lamb) curry can be turned into Sri Lankan shepherd's pie (see pic opposite, recipe on page 84). Both the curry and the shepherd's pie can be made in advance and are fine to eat a day or so after. Both can be frozen.

The papaya marinade isn't essential if you are in a hurry.

Preheat the oven to 160°C/fan 140°C/gas 3.

Put the venison chunks in a bowl. Whisk the papaya into a paste with a balloon whisk in another bowl and combine with the black pepper. Add to the venison, mix together and set aside in the fridge.

Heat 2 tablespoons of the oil in a large frying pan (with a lid) that is suitable for the oven and, when smoking, add the urry leaves followed by the onions, pandan, garlic, ginger, coriander root and green chillies, along with 1 teaspoon sea salt. Cook until the onions are soft, about 20 minutes. The more patient you are the better really, as they will get sweeter and softer the longer you cook. If the onions start to stick, you can always add a little water.

Stir the onion mix every so often. During this time, season the venison with 2 tablespoons sea salt. In a separate large pan, heat the remaining oil and, when smoking hot, brown the meat in batches, about 3 minutes on each side. Remove with a slotted spoon onto a baking tray.

Once the onions are soft and sweet, add the anchovies or fish

To serve:

1 lime, cut into wedges

Roast peanut, celery and mint
    coconut sambol (page 157)

sauce, if using, and the spices and cook for 5 minutes.

Add the meat to the curry base, along with any leftover papaya, the coconut milk, vinegar, water, sugar and cherry tomatoes. Bring to the boil with the lid off, then put the lid on the pan and put in the oven for 3 hours until the venison is tender but doesn't break up. It will separate – don't worry just stir it all together and swirl in the yoghurt, if you like. Season to taste.

Serve with lime wedges and the Peanut, celery and mint coconut sambol.

Sri Lankan shepherd's pie
ශ්‍රී ලංකා පයි

Serves 4

½ quantity venison curry
For the sweet potato mash:
6–7 (about 1.5kg) sweet potatoes
1 tbsp coconut oil
2 tsp sea salt
1 tsp chilli flakes (optional)
freshly ground black pepper,
     to taste

To serve:
Crispy onions (page 203)
handful of coriander leaves
scattering of chilli flakes
yoghurt, as desired
1 lime, cut into 4 wedges

Venison curry (see the previous page) – or lamb curry – can be turned into Sri Lankan shepherd's pie. Both the curry and the shepherd's pie can be made in advance and are fine to eat a day or so after. Both can be frozen.

Preheat the oven 180°C/fan 160°C/gas 4. Put the sweet potatoes in a roasting tin covered with tin foil and roast for 1 hour 20 minutes, or until nice and soft. Peel off the skin when still warm – this way the skin should come off easliy. Mash with a balloon whisk and add the rest of the ingredients, seasoning to taste.

Warm the curry. So that you have mostly meat and not too much juice, use a slotted spoon to spread the curry into an ovenproof dish, with the mash evenly spread on top.

Bake in the oven for 30 minutes and top with crispy onions, coriander leaves and chilli flakes. Serve with yoghurt on the side and lime wedges.

Black pork curry

කළු ඌරු මස් ව්‍යංජනි

Serves 4–6

1kg pork belly on the bone, scored with a small sharp knife

2 tbsp roasted curry powder (page 202)

freshly ground black pepper

2 tbsp coconut oil

5 red onions, 3 sliced and 2 halved

sea salt

2 tbsp fennel seeds, toasted

80g garlic, peeled and sliced

20g fresh ginger, peeled and sliced

1 bunch coriander, stalk and leaves

4–5 green chillies, roughly chopped

handful of curry leaves

2 tbsp fish sauce, plus extra to taste

1 tbsp maple syrup or kithul treacle

400ml coconut milk

1 cinnamon stick, broken in half

4 star anise

1 tbsp rose water

juice of 1 lime

To serve:

full-fat yoghurt

handful of flaked almonds

handful of pomegranate seeds

Gently slow cook pork belly on the bone and the result is really juicy, moist and melty meat with maximum flavour. Delicious the next day in a sandwich (Curry buns – page 68) or with Manioc mash (page 167) on a rainy day.

Preheat the oven to 230°C/fan 210°C/gas 8.

Rub the curry powder evenly onto the belly, along with generous amounts of freshly ground black pepper, and leave for at least 30 minutes in a clean bowl in the fridge.

Meanwhile, heat the oil in a saucepan and cook the sliced onions for 30 minutes on a low heat until they soften and sweeten. When the pork belly is ready, place skin side up in a roasting tin on top of the halved onions. Sprinkle with 2 tablespoons sea salt, add a mugful of water to create steam and roast in the oven for 20 minutes.

Place the toasted fennel seeds in a food processor with the garlic, ginger, coriander stalks, green chillies and 2 tablespoons water to create a curry paste. Add this to the sweet onions. Turn up the heat and fry for 2 minutes. Add the curry leaves, fish sauce, syrup, coconut milk, cinnamon stick and star anise. Once you have a sloppy mixture, leave to one side off the heat until your pork is ready.

Once the pork has cooked for 20 minutes, turn the oven down to 160°C/fan 140°C/gas 3. Add another mugful of water to the roasting tin and slow-cook for at least 3 hours until the meat is juicy and tender. Remove from the oven and shred carefully with two forks. Warm up the curry base and add the pork, discarding the skin and onion halves.

Add the rose water, lime juice and coriander leaves to the meat and curry base. Season to taste with salt and a little extra fish sauce. Serve with the accompaniments.

Chicken or rabbit curry

කුකුල් මස් /හා මස් ව්‍යංජන

Serves 2–4 as a side

750g chicken thighs on the bone, skin removed, or rabbit legs

sea salt and freshly ground black pepper

4 tbsp coconut oil

handful of curry leaves and chopped pandan (if you can find it)

1 tsp mustard seeds

1 tsp cumin seeds

1 red onion, peeled and thinly sliced

20g garlic, peeled and finely chopped

2–3 small green chillies, de-seeded and finely chopped

1 lemongrass stalk, bruised and finely chopped

2 spring onions, white part only, finely chopped

20g ginger, peeled and chopped fine

400ml coconut milk

200g tinned chopped tomatoes

1 tbsp light honey

1 tsp turmeric

1 cinnamon stick, broken

1 tsp chilli powder

juice of 1 lime

20g fresh coriander leaves, finely chopped

Serving suggestions:

Mango curry (page 132) or ½ fresh mango, chopped shavings of ½ coconut, toasted or raw

This curry base works well with both chicken and rabbit legs, although the rabbit likes to be cooked a little longer so the meat is falling off the bone. If using chicken, you'll need to gently peel back the skin and discard. Rabbit legs are great as they aren't covered in fat and your job is done, plus they taste better in my humble opinion. I would always choose wild rabit curry over chicken.

Season the meat in a bowl with plenty of sea salt and freshly ground black pepper.

Heat half the oil in a large wide pan and, just before it starts smoking, add the meat and brown for 5 minutes on each side.

Heat the rest of the oil in another clean heavy-based pan (with a lid). Just before it starts to smoke, add the curry leaves and pandan followed by the mustard seeds and cumin seeds. The mustard should crackle and pop immediately. Turn down the heat and quickly add the onion, garlic, ginger, green chillies, lemongrass, spring onions and 1 teaspoon sea salt. Fry for 5 minutes or so, stirring every now and again.

Once the onion has softened, add the rest of the spices, then the chicken or rabbit followed by the coconut milk, tomatoes, honey, turmeric, cinnamon and chilli powder. If using chicken, simmer for 30 minutes with the lid off to reduce the sauce and deepen the flavour. If cooking rabbit legs, add 100ml water and bring to the boil, then simmer with the lid on for 1 ½ hours. Once you are happy that the meat is juicy and tender, check the sauce for seasoning and tweak accordingly. Stir in the lime juice and chopped coriander.

Tip: I sometimes spoon leftover cooked rice into this dish – allow it to soak up the juices for a few minutes and you have a ready-made, instant one-pot wonder risotto/paella-type thing. You can do this with most meat curries.

Kottu rottu

කොත්තු රොටී

Serves 4

1 quantity meat curry, preferably
   chicken/rabbit (page 86)

3 large eggs

2–3 large soft tortillas or
   gothamba roti

2 tbsp coconut oil

150g leeks, finely sliced

150g carrots, washed and grated

150g cabbage, shredded

1 red onion, finely chopped

20g garlic, peeled and
   finely chopped

20g fresh ginger, peeled and
   finely chopped

handful of curry leaves

2–3 small green chillies, chopped

1 tsp cumin seeds

1 tsp turmeric

1 cinnamon stick, broken

2 spring onions, white part
   only, finely chopped

1 small bunch coriander, washed
   and roots finely chopped

sea salt and freshly ground
   black pepper

To serve:

4 spring onions, thinly sliced

crushed peanuts (optional)

coriander leaves

At about 5pm, the soundtrack of loud-clanging steel blades chopping the Kottu rottu in harmonious rhythm at little cramped vendors across Sri Lanka is a delight to see and hear.

This dish is quite literally banging. A great way to mix things up from the usual rice and curry, and one of my favourite recipes in the book. It is the country's most popular street food; proper comfort food and great for a hangover or late-night munchies. Sri Lankans use Gothamba roti, but here I use tortilla as a substitute. It softens to a tagliatelle pasta consistency and is very moreish.

Heat the meat curry. Separate the curry sauce, cover to ensure it stays warm and put to one side. Strip the meat off the bone with gloves if you have any, or clean hands, and put aside.

Lightly beat the eggs with a pinch of salt and pepper in a separate bowl, and cut your tortillas or roti into thin strips that resemble tagliatelle so everything is good to go.

Heat the oil in a large frying pan or wok on a high heat. Add everything, apart from the meat and curry sauce, eggs and tortilla/roti strips, along with 1 teaspoon salt and some black pepper. Fry for 5 minutes, stirring all the time.

Then add the tortilla or roti followed by the meat and beaten eggs. Cook for 2 minutes then check the seasoning and serve immediately with the sliced spring onions, crushed peanuts, if using, coriander leaves and then stir in as much warm curry sauce as you like, depending how dry or 'wet' you like it. I like it quite sloppy.

Roast spiced chicken with brown sugar, limes and coconut milk

දුඹුරු සිනි දෙහි ගෙඩි සමග

Serves 4

2kg free-range chicken

½ quantity Chilli butter
    (page 218), melted

800ml coconut milk

sea salt and freshly ground
    black pepper

For the marinade:

500g natural yoghurt or curd

50g fresh ginger, peeled and
    roughly chopped

50g garlic, peeled

1 tbsp chilli powder

1 tbsp turmeric

1 tbsp freshly ground black pepper

For the brown sugar limes:

4 limes

2 tbsp coconut oil, melted

2 tbsp brown sugar or
    grated jaggery

To serve:

chopped fresh herbs

pomegranate seeds

Serving suggestions:

vegetable curries (pages 113–137)

Gotu kola (page 146)

Coconut sambal (page 154)

Make this if you want to impress and spice up Sunday lunch. The butter, coconut milk and chicken juices turn into a gutsy sauce. Spatchcocking quickens the cooking time and ensures the chicken is cooked evenly – even in a dodgy oven. Marinating the bird in yoghurt tenderises the meat, making it extra juicy and succulent.

First, make the marinade. Whizz everything in a blender, or grate the ginger and garlic into a bowl and combine with the yoghurt and spices using a wooden spoon.

Next, spatchcock the chicken. Turn it over onto its back with its head facing towards you. Cut down each side of the chicken along the spine with strong kitchen scissors, then turn the chicken over and press down hard on the breast with both hands until you have flattened the chicken. Alternatively, you could ask your butcher to do this.

Cover the chicken with the marinade, inside and out. Leave overnight in the fridge or for at least a couple of hours.

Preheat the oven to 200°C/fan 180°C/gas 6 and find a roasting tin that allows the chicken to fit snugly inside. Remove the chicken from the fridge, shake off a little of the excess marinade and then spread the chilli butter all over the surface of the bird. It doesn't matter if it is not evenly spread as it will melt naturally into the coconut sauce. Season generously all over with 2 teaspoons sea salt and plenty of freshly ground black pepper.

cont.

Meanwhile, cut the limes in half and put in a bowl. Mix in the oil and sugar and place skin side down on a baking tray with most of the sugar on the flesh. Place on the top shelf of the oven in the last 20 minutes of cooking.

Check the chicken is cooked by slicing the skin between the leg and the breast and seeing if the juices run clear.
If so, the chicken is ready.

Put the chicken juices and coconut milk that remain in the tin through a sieve and season to taste with more salt or brown sugar if necessary. Transfer the chicken to a warm serving plate and leave to rest for at least 20 and up to 40 minutes uncovered, then serve it with the sieved sauce, the brown sugar limes, some chopped fresh herbs and pomegranate seeds and any of the optional serving suggestions.

Beef curry

හරක් මස් ව්‍යංජන

Serves 4

1kg blade of beef or beef shin, cubed

2 tbsp roasted curry powder (page 202)

3–5 tbsp coconut oil

2 red onions, finely chopped

1 tsp sea salt

4 Ortiz anchovies, roughly chopped, or 30g Maldive fish flakes

handful of curry leaves

handful of fresh fenugreek leaves or 1 tsp toasted and ground fenugreek seeds

5cm pandan (if you have any)

20g garlic, peeled and finely chopped

20g fresh ginger, peeled and finely chopped

1 tsp chilli powder

1 cinnamon stick, broken in half

4 cloves

2 small red bird's-eye chillies, deseeded and chopped

400g tinned chopped tomatoes

To serve:

fresh yoghurt

raw oysters

handful of coriander leaves

A traditional Sri Lankan beef curry should bring out little beads of sweat on your forehead, but you can make it as spicy as you like.

Good-quality meat is hard to find in Sri Lanka. The majority of the population is either Buddhist or Hindu and therefore beef isn't that popular. In the UK, try to get dry-aged beef, as this process concentrates the meat and intensifies the flavour and texture. You can buy fresh fenugreek (I get mine from asiancookshop.co.uk), but don't worry if you haven't got any – as an alternative, you can toast and grind a teaspoon of fenugreek seeds. This curry can be frozen.

Put the meat in a bowl with the curry powder and mix together well, then set aside in a fridge or somewhere cool to marinate. The longer you can marinate the meat, the better really, but 30 minutes is fine if in a hurry.

Preheat the oven to 160°C/fan 140°C/gas 3.

Heat 3 tablespoons of the oil in a large pan and brown the meat in batches. Don't overcrowd the pan. Remove the meat and set aside (keep the oil if fairly clean and not burnt).

Heat the retained meat oil or 2 tablespoons fresh oil in a separate pan that can also go in the oven. Sweat the onions for 15 minutes with the salt and anchovies or Maldive fish flakes. Then add the browned meat, curry leaves and fenugreek, as well as the pandan, garlic, ginger, chilli powder, cinnamon, cloves and red chillies. Cover with 200ml water and the chopped tomatoes. Bring to the boil.

Transfer to the oven for at least 3 hours, until the meat is soft, tender and juicy. The sauce should have mostly evaporated. Give it a big stir and check the seasoning. Serve with the coriander leaves scattered over.

Biryani

බුරියානි

Serves 4

300g red rice or white basmati

150g salted butter

10 curry leaves (if possible)

2 red onions, thinly sliced

2 tsp sea salt

10cm pandan (if possible)

6cm lemongrass, white part
    only, thinly sliced

2 green chillies, thinly sliced

20g garlic, peeled and thinly sliced

2 cinnamon sticks, broken in half

2 tsp turmeric

4 cardamon pods, bruised

100g cashew nuts, chopped

50g raisins or currants

3 tsp good-quality rose
    water (optional)

1 quantity meat curry of
    choice (I prefer lamb's
    neck or pig's cheek)

To serve:

rose water, for sprinkling

curry toppings of your
    choice (page 203) plain
    full-fat yoghurt

yoghurt, as desired

chopped fresh coriander

pomegranate seeds

Proper lime and soda (page
    196 – optional)

This looks and tastes mega and is a real treat to have on a special occasion. I particularly like using white rice or string hoppers, as they turn a brilliant bright yellow from the turmeric, contrasting wonderfully with the rich dark meat, dollops of cooling white yoghurt, fresh green coriander and stained glass pink pomegranate jewels.

Try it with ice cold Proper lime and soda flavoured with rose and cinnamon.

Soak the rice in cold water for at least 30 minutes but up to 2 hours.

Melt the butter in a large saucepan (with a lid) and add the curry leaves until they crackle, then the onions, half the salt, the pandan and lemongrass. Turn down the heat and cook for 30 minutes until the onions are very soft. In the last 10 minutes of cooking, add the chillies and garlic, followed by the spices, and fry for a couple of minutes. Then add the nuts and raisins and cook for 5 minutes on a high heat, stirring all the time.

Boil the kettle with 600ml water. Drain the rice and add to the pan with the remaining salt. Stir so everything is nicely coated. Pour in the boiled water, stir again and bring to the boil. Put on the lid and turn down the heat. Cook gently for 10 minutes on a low heat. Take off the heat and leave to steam for 10 minutes. It will keep warm for at least half an hour, if not more.

When ready to serve, fluff up with a fork and add a sprinkle of rose water, if you like. Adjust the seasoning. Now for the layering!

Warm up your choice of meat curry. Spoon a third of the rice onto a large dish followed by half the meat curry, then another third on top of that, the rest of the meat curry then the last third of the rice. Put in the oven at 180°C/fan 160°C/gas 4 for 10 minutes so all the juices seep into the rice but the biryani still keeps its identity. Sprinkle with rose water, garnish with any of the curry toppings and serve with yoghurt, fresh coriander and pomegranate seeds.

String hopper biryani

250g dried string hoppers or rice vermicelli noodles

same ingredients as above except:
100g salted butter instead of 150g
1 tsp sea salt instead of 2
handful of coriander leaves, chopped

Instead of using rice, soak the string hoppers or rice noodles in boiling water for 3 minutes, then drain and leave in a large bowl while you prepare the biryani sauce, following the method above.

Once the buttery, onion spice mix is done, tip into the large bowl with the string hoppers or noodles and, using tongs, gently combine the two. Stir through the coriander leaves then layer up as above. This is also really nice without the meat curry, served with chopped herbs and fresh pineapple pickle (page 213).

3.2
FISH

මාළු

Ambul thiyal

ඇඹුල්තියල්

Serves 2–4 as a side
to a rice dish and curry feast

500g fresh tuna steaks

1 tsp chilli powder

2 tbsp roasted curry
    powder (page 202)

1 tsp freshly ground black pepper

1 tbsp vegetable or coconut oil

handful of curry leaves

5g pandan (if you can find it)

2 small red onions, thinly sliced

1–2 green bird's-eye chillies,
    de-seeded and sliced

10g fresh ginger, peeled and sliced

10g garlic, peeled and sliced

1 tsp sea salt, plus extra pinch

1 tbsp tamarind paste

1 cinnamon stick, broken in half

squeeze of lime juice

To serve:

handful of coriander leaves

1 lime, cut into wedges

sliced avocado and green
    salad (optional)

I've never seen such gigantic tuna as you get along the south coast of Sri Lanka, the size of a small cow and cut clean with a machete right in front of you. It's unlike anything you will ever see or taste in the UK.

Ambul thiyal is a dry, sour and spicy curry. Goraka – a yellow fruit that turns black and sour when sun dried and is traditionally used in the dish – is cooked in a clay pot, giving a slightly smoky, tangy flavour which helps preserve the fish. A hangover from the days of no refrigeration, goraka can be hard to find in the UK so I have replaced it with lime juice, tamarind and ginger. I like tuna to be tender and juicy, so I only cook for a couple of minutes on a high heat so the fish is just cooked.

Chop the tuna into 3cm pieces and marinate with the chilli powder, curry powder and black pepper. Set aside.

Heat the oil in a saucepan and, when beginning to smoke, add the curry leaves followed by the pandan, onions, green chillies, ginger and garlic. Season with the salt. Fry for a couple of minutes then add the fish and 2 tablespoons water, the tamarind paste, cinnamon and a big pinch of salt. Stir and cook on a high heat for a minute then add a squeeze of lime juice.

Serve with coriander leaves and lime wedges, with some sliced avocado and a green salad, if you like.

Squid curry

දැල්ලා ව්‍යංජනයි

Serves 4–6 as a side dish

500g squid

3 tbsp coconut oil

handful of curry leaves
     (if possible)

1 red onion, peeled and
     thinly sliced

1–2 small green chillies,
     deseeded and chopped

15g garlic, peeled and thinly sliced

handful of coriander root,
     chopped and leaves

1 tsp sea salt, plus extra pinch

2 tsp roasted curry powder
     (page 202)

1 tsp turmeric

½ tsp chilli powder

1 cinnamon stick

400ml coconut milk

3 tsp kithul treacle or maple syrup

juice of 1 lime

2 tbsp fish sauce

So that the squid is juicy, melty and tender, cook it using a very hot, wide pan to give it lots of space – don't overcrowd or flip it over. Cook it one side only. You could use the same method for prawns or mackerel (see tip below).

Ask your fishmonger to kindly clean and gut the squid. Separate the wings and cut the body into long strips 3cm wide, then cut again in half. Cut the tentacles in half.

Heat 2 tablespoons of the coconut oil in saucepan and, once smoking, add the curry leaves, quickly followed by the onion, chillies, garlic and coriander root. Season with the salt and fry for 5 minutes so that the onions caramelise and then add the spices. Stir for a couple of minutes then add the coconut milk and treacle or syrup, 100ml water, lime juice, fish sauce and a pinch of salt. Simmer for a couple of minutes.

Heat the remaining coconut oil in a separate large frying or griddle pan and, when just about to smoke, add the squid, in batches if you have to – try to make sure they don't touch each other, otherwise they will not char. Cook for a couple of minutes on one side then add to the warm coconut sauce taken off the heat.

Adjust the seasoning, then serve.

Tip – Turn the above into Fried mackerel curry – frying rather poaching ensures the fish remains intact and adds a lovely smoky flavour and contrast in texture. Heat 2 tbsp coconut oil in a large frying or griddle pan and fry 1kg mackerel fillets skin side down with plenty of freshly ground black pepper for 4–5 minutes until the flesh is mostly cooked. Add the mackerel to the coconut gravy instead of the squid. Turn the heat off and baste the fish with the warm sauce and it will cook perfectly. This is very nice with tomato salad with lots of mint and coriander.

Sprats curry

හාල්මැස්ස වියංජනි

Serves 4–6 as a side dish

800g sardines, sprats, fresh
    anchovies or large whitebait

2 tbsp coconut oil

handful of curry leaves

200g red onions, peeled
    and thinly sliced

15g garlic, peeled and thinly sliced

1 red chilli

1 tsp cumin seeds

1 tsp fenugreek

1 tsp fennel seeds

1 tsp sea salt, plus extra pinch

1 tsp turmeric

1 tsp chilli powder

400ml coconut milk/100ml water

150g vine tomatoes, halved

4–5 anchovies, chopped

juice of ½ lime

There is an abundance of fresh wild fish caught every morning in Sri Lanka; Kingfish, Trevally, Snapper, Grouper, Swordfish, Shark, Tuna, Crab, Squid, Sprats and Spanish Mackerel are the most commonly used for curries.

I first made Sprats curry at the Devon home of my friends Rose and Daisy, by the British seaside. I prefer making this curry with sardines as the bones are a bit easier to manage than those of sprats. You could use a mix of any of the fish listed.

First clean the fish. I like to keep the heads on but you might like to take them off.

Heat the coconut oil in a large saucepan (with a lid) and, once smoking, add the curry leaves, quickly followed by the onions, garlic, red chilli, cumin, fenugreek and fennel seeds. Season with the salt and fry for 5 minutes so that the onions caramelise, then add the turmeric and chilli powder. Stir for a couple of minutes.

Add the coconut milk or water, tomatoes, anchovies, lime juice and a pinch of salt. Simmer for a couple of minutes then add the fish and bring to the boil. Remove from the heat, popping the lid on the pan. Let the fish cook in its own heat for 5 minutes before serving.

Fishball curry

මාළු කටිලට ව්‍යංජනය

Serves 2–4 as a side dish

700g skinless fish (a mix
  of salmon, smoked
  haddock and/or cod)

½ small red onion, finely chopped

zest of 1 lime and juice of ½

20g garlic, finely chopped

2–3 small green chilies, deseeded
  and finely chopped

sea salt and freshly ground
  black pepper

50g breadcrumbs (I use
  Panko but whatever
  you can get hold of)

2 tbsp vegetable or coconut oil

handful of curry leaves
  (if possible)

400ml coconut milk

1 tsp roasted curry powder
  (page 202)

1 tsp chilli powder

½ tsp turmeric

coriander leaves, to garnish

Serving suggestions:

rice (page 168) or string
  hopper pilau (page 164)

2 or 3 vegetable curries
  (pages 114–37)

Gotu Kola (page 146)

Derived from the Portuguese. These fishballs are smoky, juicy and lightly spiced contrasting perfectly with the creamy, mild and slightly sweet warm sauce.

If you want to go gluten-free you could add an egg for a bit of security instead of the breadcrumbs. However, breadcrumbs give a very nice light texture as well as keeping the fishballs together.

This curry can be frozen.

Mince the fish in a blender into a coarse paste and then add the onion, lime zest, garlic and chillies with 1 ½ teaspoons sea salt and 1 tsp freshly ground black pepper. Blend again for a second or two, then stir in the breadcrumbs. Shape the mixture into balls about 4cm in diameter and set aside.

Heat the oil in a large wide pan and, when smoking, add the curry leaves if you have any. Then add the fishballs and brown for a couple of minutes each side. Don't turn over too soon or they will stick to the pan and break up – when they are ready they will move easily with kitchen tongs.

Once all your fishballs are browned, heat the coconut milk in a separate saucepan (with a lid) with the spices. Bring up to a simmer with ½ teaspoon salt and add the fishballs. Take the pan off the heat and leave to cook in the warm liquid with the lid on for 5 minutes. Then stir in the lime juice and garnish with coriander leaves.

Serve with rice or String hopper pilau and a selection of vegetable curries or salad.

Devilled prawns or Monkfish curry

ඉස්සන් බැදුම

This is essentially quite messy but, depending on your attitude, is quite fun getting your fingers sticky and juicy. In Sri Lanka prawns are often cooked in the shells as that is where the flavour is – like cooking meat on the bone. It's nice for the prawn to keep a bit of identity and keep its shell too.

Monkfish holds very well and, like prawns, is sweet and juicy. Perfect for a rich tomato, saffron curry. You could also use another firm fish like red mullet or lobster. Leftover fish curry a bit watered down makes a good fish soup!

Get a saucepan and sweat the onions with 2 tablespoons coconut oil and 1 teaspoon salt in a large saucepan for 20 minutes until nice and soft. Add the ginger, red chili and garlic followed by the spices. Cook for 5 minutes then add the chopped tomatoes, 50ml water and optional fish sauce and the sugar. Simmer for 10 minutes to thicken and reduce.

Get a frying pan and fry the prawns (if using) in a smoking pan of 1 tablespoon of coconut oil for 3 minutes on each side until charred and pink. Set aside.

Add the coconut milk and lime juice to the sauce, adjust the seasoning and simmer for another 5 minutes then add the prawns or monkfish, depending on which you're using, and turn off the heat. Put on the lid and let steam and cook in its heat for 10 minutes or so.

Serve with rice and vegetable curries or make into a Poppadom fish pie (page 109).

Serves 4–6 as a side

2 red onion, thinly sliced

3 tbsp coconut oil

15g fresh ginger, grated

2 red chillis, de-seeded and finely chopped

15g garlic, finely chopped

1 cinnamon stick

1 tsp turmeric

1 big pinch saffron threads

1 tsp chilli powder

2 tsp smoked paprika

400g tin of chopped tomato

2 tbsp fish sauce (optional)

1 tb brown sugar or jaggery

400ml coconut milk

sea salt

black pepper

1kg (about 16) raw jumbo prawns in their shells or monkfish fillet, chopped into 4cm (ish) even size chunks

½ lime, juice

Serving suggestions:
rice (page 168)
2 or 3 vegetable curries
(pages 114–37)

Poppadom fish pie

පපඩම් මාළු පයි

Serves 4

1 x Monkfish curry
(page 106)

8 large cooked poppadom,
crushed with hands

100g grated cheddar cheese

1 tsp smoked paprika

1 tsp turmeric

4 limes, cut into wedges

For the fresh coriander chutney:

50g washed bunch of coriander,
leaves and stalk

1 green chilli

75g rapeseed oil

pinch of salt

½ lime, juice

To serve:

lime wedges

a vegetable curry (pages 114–37)

green salad

My mum makes fish pie with cornflakes - and this is inspired by that. If you have time, you could make it with a layer of okra curry, fried potato or fried leeks

Preheat the oven to 180°C/fan 160°C/gas 4. Place the monkfish curry in a large ovenproof dish.

Get a large bowl and crush up the poppadoms with your hands. You don't want a dust but you also don't want the pieces to be too large and spikey. Add the grated cheese, paprika and turmeric and mix well. Place evenly on top of the curry, then transfer to the middle shelf of the oven. Cook for 30 minutes until the poppadom is golden, the curry is bubbling and the cheese has melted.

While the fish pie is in the oven, prepare the coriander chutney. Place all the ingredients in a blender until the consistency is nice and smooth, or use a pestle and mortar.

When the fish pie is ready, remove from the oven and leave to cool for 10 minutes or so before serving. Dollop spoonfuls of coriander chutney on top of the pie and serve with lime wedges, a vegetable curry and green salad.

Spiced roast bass in banana leaf

Serves 4–6

500g whole fresh sea bass from your fishmonger, scaled and gutted (head left on)

1 small bunch coriander, washed

1 small onion, sliced

20g garlic, peeled

3–4cm piece fresh ginger

4cm lemongrass, white part only, chopped

2 green chillies, deseeded and chopped

½ tsp cinnamon

2 tsp sea salt

freshly ground black pepper, to taste

handful of curry leaves

4–5cm pandan (optional)

2 tbsp chilli butter (page 218) or salted butter

1 lime, halved

¼ small banana leaf,

To serve:

1 lime, cut into wedges

handful of coriander leaves

fried chard (optional, page 162)

Coconut oil and lime mayo (optional, page 206)

Serving suggestions:

Gotu Kola (page 146)

Cucumber curry (page 125)

Rice (page 168)

Fried leeks or chard (page 162)

Sharing a whole fish on the bone roasted in banana leaf, with a selection of curries, on the beach. Waves crashing at sunset against rocks and willowy palm trees. The ideal set-up.

If you don't have a beach or a sea bass, you can roast individual mullet, smaller-size bass or bream this way. Unlike Sri Lanka, where it is available in abundance, it can be a challenge to find good-quality, reasonable-value wild fish in the UK – always buy your fish at the fish counter or from your local fishmonger. For banana leaves, look in Asian shops or online at asiancookshop.co.uk, or alternatively you could use baking paper and wrap it up with string like a parcel.

This is moist, juicy and smells as good as it tastes. Delicious with fried chard and lovely with dollops of Coconut and lime mayo.

Preheat the oven to 200°C/fan 180°C/gas 6.

Use a sharp knife to cut diagonal slashes in the flesh of the fish about 2–3cm apart.

Chop the ends off the coriander and put them and all the remaining ingredients – except the coriander leaves (kept on the stalk), lime and banana leaf – in a food processor and blend, or bash up in a pestle and mortar. Rub the mixture over the fish's body, pushing it into all the grooves. Shove the coriander stalks and leaves in the body cavity. Squeeze the juice of the lime all over the fish and put the lime skins inside the cavity too.

Wrap the fish in banana leaf (or baking paper). Place in the oven or on a barbecue for 10 minutes on each side until just cooked. Serve with lime wedges and scatter with coriander leaves.

3.3

VEG & FRUIT

එළවළු සහ පලතුරු

Basic vegetable curry

මූලික එළවළු ව්‍යංජන

Serves 4

1 tbsp vegetable or coconut oil

handful of curry leaves
(if possible)

1 tsp black mustard seeds

1 tsp cumin seeds

1 red onion, finely sliced

1 tsp sea salt

20g garlic, peeled and finely sliced

20g fresh ginger, peeled and
finely chopped (optional)

2–3 green or red chillies, deseeded and finely
chopped

1 small bunch coriander stalks,
finely chopped (optional)

1 cinnamon stick, broken

1 tsp turmeric

200ml coconut milk

50ml water or 200g tinned
chopped tomatoes

*Choice of spices (choose 2–4 on
top of curry powder):*

roasted curry powder (page 202)

1 tsp fenugreek seeds

4 cloves

5 cardamom pods

1 tsp chilli powder

Choice of vegetable:

450g different varieties (e.g.
pumpkin, potato, cauliflower,
cabbage, mushrooms,
kale) or fruit – try 500g
papaya or pineapple

To serve:

juice of 1 lime

handful of coriander leaves

*This is like the meat curry base, but I stir-fry the onions quickly
on a very high heat in order to char and caramelise rather than
slow-cook and soften.*

*Sri Lankans tend to leave ginger out of vegetable dishes and save
it for meat and fish curries, but you can add if you like. Make sure
you prep all your ingredients first so everything is organised and
good to go.*

Heat the oil in a heavy-based pan and, just before it starts to
smoke, add the curry leaves followed by the mustard seeds
and cumin seeds. The mustard seeds should crackle and pop
immediately. Turn down the heat (otherwise your mustard
seeds will burn and become bitter) and quickly add the onion
and salt.

Add the garlic, ginger (if using), chillies and coriander stalks,
if you like. Cook for 2 minutes, then add the cinnamon stick,
turmeric and spices of your choice, cook for 2 minutes then
add the vegetable of your choice. Stir so that everything is
nicely coated in the oil, spices and garlic mix. Then add the
coconut milk and water or tomatoes. Simmer, uncovered, for
30 minutes, stirring occasionally, until the vegetable is cooked
– add 2 tablespoons water if it starts to stick to the bottom of
the pan.

Serve with a squeeze of lime juice and a scattering of
coriander leaves.

Cashew curry

කජු කරි

Serves 4–6 as a side

1 tbsp coconut oil

handful of curry leaves
    (if possible)

1 red onion, thinly sliced

10g garlic, peeled and thinly sliced

1–2 green bird's eye chillies,
    deseeded and thinly sliced

sea salt

1 tsp roasted curry powder
    (page 202)

1 cinnamon stick, broken in half

1 tsp turmeric

400ml coconut milk

300g whole blanched cashew
    nuts soaked in cold water
    for 2 hours, then drained

4 anchovies, chopped, or 1 tbsp
    fish sauce (optional)

75g kale, green beans or peas

juice of ½ lime

½ tsp chilli flakes

Serving suggestions:

any vegetable curry
    (pages 114–137)

rice (page 168)

Gotu kola (page 146)

Cashew curry is pretty decadent and satisfying for a vegetarian curry and very popular in Sri Lanka where cashews grow on trees – the cashew nut is actually a seed growing in the stem of the cashew apple. The green vegetable could be anything seasonal to provide a bit of colour, freshness and texture.
I like this version with kale in the winter, but in summer you could use green beans (snake beans in Sri Lanka) or frozen peas instead. Greens like spinach, cabbage, chard and kale all work well.

This is fine eaten the next day but is best fresh. Do not freeze.

Heat the oil in a medium-sized saucepan (with a lid) and, when hot, add the curry leaves quickly followed by the onion, garlic, chillies and 1 teaspoon sea salt. Fry for a couple of minutes then add the spices. Stir for a minute or so then add the coconut milk and drained cashews. Simmer for 5 minutes and add the anchovies or fish sauce, if using.

Meanwhile, steam your veg and then add to the curry. Or I usually just cook it in the residual heat of the pan, with the lid on, once the curry is cooked. Then add the lime juice and chilli flakes and season to taste with salt.

Garlic curry

සුදුළුණු ව්‍යංජන

Serves 2–4 as a side

1 tbsp coconut oil

handful of curry leaves
    (if possible)

200g shallots, peeled and
    thinly sliced

½ tsp sea salt

350g garlic, cloves peeled
    but left whole

15g fresh ginger, peeled
    and chopped

2 bird's eye green chillies

1 tsp turmeric

1 cinnamon stick, broken

½ tsp chilli powder

200ml coconut milk

1 tsp freshly ground black pepper

1 tsp brown sugar or jaggery

5 anchovies, chopped

pinch of saffron threads (optional)

100g tinned chopped tomatoes

50g wild garlic (if available) or
    spinach leaves (optional)

Serving suggestions:
stir-fried broccoli
Chicken curry (page 86)
any meat or fish curry
Pol roti for Sri Lankan
    'bruschetta' (page 32)
rice (page 168)

I first tried sticky garlic curry in the beautiful hill country around Ella. The little, cooked garlic cloves remind me of gnocchi and, when slow-cooked, they mellow in flavour into sweet garlic dumplings. I like to add a few leaves of wild garlic in the spring. The fresher the garlic cloves, the better. Old garlic will taste stale and bitter. Asian garlic is smaller in the UK, which is why I refer to amounts in grams rather than cloves. If you want to cheat, I know Whole Foods sell peeled garlic.

This curry goes beautifully with plenty of things (see serving suggestions for ideas), but it also loves to be slathered on Pol roti and baked in the oven, like a Sri Lankan-style bruschetta.

This can be made ahead of time and is fine to eat a couple of days after. Do not freeze.

Heat the oil in a medium-sized saucepan and, once hot, add the curry leaves then turn down the heat and sweat the shallots with the salt for 10–15 minutes, stirring every now and again to prevent them sticking. You can always add a tablespoon of water if your shallots do start to stick.

Once the shallots are soft, sweet and caramelised, add the garlic cloves, ginger, whole green chillies and 100ml water and cook for another 5 minutes. Add the turmeric, cinnamon and chilli powder, stir and cook for a couple of minutes then add the coconut milk, black pepper, brown sugar, anchovies and saffron, if using. Cook on a low heat for 10 minutes then add the tomatoes and 100ml water and cook for another 10 minutes until the garlic is sweet, soft and sticky. Add wild garlic leaves if you have any, or spinach, if you like. No lime in this one.

Beetroot curry

බ‍ීට්‍රූට්

Serves 4–6 as a side

3 tbsp vegetable or coconut oil

10 curry leaves (if possible)

3cm pandan, finely chopped
(if you have any)

1 tsp black mustard seeds

1 tsp cumin seeds

1 red onion, finely sliced

2 small red chillies, finely sliced

20g fresh ginger, peeled and
finely chopped

20g garlic, peeled and thinly sliced

1 cinnamon stick, broken

1 tsp chilli powder

500g small raw red beetroots or
carrots, washed, peeled and
cut into batons (save the
leaves and stems for a salad)

150g tomatoes, roughly chopped

200ml coconut milk

1 tbsp soft brown sugar

juice of ½ lime

sea salt

To serve:

buffalo curd or seasoned
full-fat yoghurt

lime wedges

fresh mint leaves or dill sprigs

Serving suggestions:

selection of curries: Squid curry
(page 100); Beef curry
(page 93), Cucumber
curry (page 125), Spiced
roast bass (page 110)

Gotu kola (page 146)

Sweet, earthy, lightly spiced and beautifully bright pink. Lovely served warm with the fried mackerel version of Squid curry (page 100), or cold with creamy ripe avocado and crumbled goat's cheese. You could use carrots instead of beetroot to make a bright orange carrot curry – add a couple of cardamom pods if you do. This can be made in advance and is fine to eat a day or so after. It can also be frozen.

As with every curry, first prepare your vegetables so you can chuck it all in and your job is super-easy. I always wear latex gloves when preparing the beetroot so as not to stain hands with beetroot juice.

Heat the oil in a heavy-based pan (with a lid) and, just before it starts to smoke, add the curry leaves and pandan, and then the mustard and cumin seeds. The mustard should crackle and pop immediately. Turn down the heat and quickly add the onion, chilli, ginger and garlic and fry for a couple of minutes, seasoned with 1 teaspoon sea salt.

Stir in the cinnamon and chilli powder and cook for a few seconds then add the beetroot, tomatoes, coconut milk, sugar and 1 teaspoon sea salt. Bring to the boil, cover and lower the heat. Cook for 15–20 minutes until the beetroot is tender but slightly crunchy. Stir in the lime juice and check the seasoning. Serve with a dollop of buffalo curd or seasoned yoghurt, lime wedges and fresh mint or dill.

Tip – Beetroot curry can be made into spiced beetroot dip served with poppadoms for a canapé or starter. Remove the pandan and cinnamon stick from the sauce and whizz up the cooked beetroot without the cooking liquid in a blender with 1 tablespoon plain full-fat yoghurt. Adjust the seasoning with salt and lime juice.

Okra curry

බණ්ඩක්කා කරි

Serves 4

500g okra, washed and trimmed

about 100ml vegetable oil,
    for deep-frying

2 tbsp coconut oil

handful of curry leaves
    (if possible)

1 tsp mustard seeds

1 tsp cumin seeds

75g red onion, thinly sliced

20g coriander root, washed
    and finely chopped

2 small green chillies, deseeded
    and finely chopped

15g garlic, peeled and thinly sliced

115g cherry tomatoes, halved
    (I like to use Datterini)

2–3 anchovies, finely chopped

150ml coconut milk

1 tsp sea salt

juice of ½ lime

½ tsp chilli powder

1 tsp turmeric

1 tsp roasted curry powder
    (page 202)

1 tsp fish sauce, 1 tsp maple
    surup, kithul treacle
    (to taste, optional)

People go on about okra being slimy. I don't mind this but I do like a bit of texture and crunch. Gently frying beforehand means you avoid the slime and sludge problem. Choose small, straight, green okra as these are fresh and less bitter. If you have any leftover okra curry, try it in a salad with green leaves, pomegranate seeds and lots of fresh herbs.

This keeps well for a few days and can be frozen.

Cut the okra in half and put in a bowl.

Get two saucepans. Heat the oil for deep-frying in one pan, ensuring that you have a depth of 4cm oil, and, once hot, fry the okra for 12 minutes until crisp, stirring occasionally.

Meanwhile, heat the coconut oil in the second pan and, when almost smoking, add the curry leaves, mustard and cumin seeds until the mustard seeds pop. Then add the onion, coriander root, chillies, garlic, tomatoes and anchovies. Stir for a couple of minutes then add the spices, followed by the coconut milk and salt. Cook for 5 minutes then stir in the lime juice. Adjust the seasoning to taste with fish sauce, maple syrup or kithult treacle, if you life.

Drain the okra from the oil and add to the sauce, cook for a couple of minutes then serve.

Sweet potato curry

 බතල ව්‍යංජන

Serves 4 –6 as a side

750g sweet potatoes, peeled and chopped into even-sized pieces

3 tbsp coconut oil

sea salt

1 tsp roasted curry powder (page 202)

½ tsp turmeric

¼ tsp grated nutmeg

½ tsp ground cinnamon

½ tsp chilli powder

1 tsp mustard seeds

handful of curry leaves and chopped pandan (if you have any)

100g red onion, thinly sliced

2 green chillies, deseeded and chopped

15g garlic, peeled and finely chopped

100ml water

1 tbsp brown sugar

150ml coconut milk

a squeeze of lime juice

freshly ground black pepper

Marinating and roasting root vegetables brings out the sweetness of the vegetable, adds a deeper, smokier flavour and texture and helps retain the shape. You could also make this dish using celeriac, turnip or parsnip.

Leftovers of this very versatile dry curry are great as a layer in Tomato curry 'shakshuka' (page 40); whizzed into a soup; mashed as a topping for Sri Lankan shepherd's pie (page 84); or a base to Poppadom fish pie (page 109). It also keeps well for a few days and can be frozen.

Preheat the oven to 200°C/fan 180°C/gas 6. In a bowl combine the sweet potatoes with 2 tablespoons of the coconut oil, 2 teaspoons sea salt and the spices (except for the mustard seeds). Cover a baking tray with baking paper (so the spices don't stick to the bottom) and spread the mix evenly onto the tray. Put in the oven and roast for at least 45 minutes or until the potatoes are nice and soft.

Heat the remaining coconut oil in a large saucepan and, when just starting to smoke, add the mustard seeds, curry leaves and pandan, followed by the onion, chillies and garlic. Season with salt. Fry for a couple of minutes then add the water, 1 teaspoon salt, the sugar and coconut milk and simmer for 10 minutes. Take the sweet potatoes out of the oven and add to the sauce. Stir and simmer for a couple of minutes until most of the liquid has been absorbed. Stir in a squeeze of lime juice and adjust the seasoning to taste.

Roast cauliflower curry

I could eat this most days of the week. Good thing, as cauliflowers always seem to be in the shops. Best eaten as served. Do not freeze.

Serves 4

1kg cauliflower or romanesco head, roughly chopped into similar-size florets

50ml sesame oil

1 tsp sea salt

1 tsp turmeric

¼ tsp cayenne pepper

freshly ground black pepper

2 tbsp peanuts

zest of 1 lime and juice of ½

handful of coriander leaves, finely chopped

handful of mint, finely chopped

30g raisins (optional)

Preheat the oven to 200°C/fan 180°C/gas 6.

Place the cauliflower florets in a large bowl with the sesame oil, salt, turmeric, cayenne and plenty of freshly ground black pepper. Mix well to make sure everything is evenly covered. Place the cauliflower mix on a baking tray lined with baking paper (not tin foil otherwise it will stick) and roast for 30 minutes on the top shelf until the cauliflower is golden and a little charred.

While the cauliflower is roasting, crush the peanuts lightly in a pestle and mortar and then mix with the cauliflower for the last 5 minutes of cooking time.

When the cauliflower is golden brown, remove from the oven and put into a cool dish. Add the lime zest and juice and scatter over the fresh herbs and raisins, if using.

TIP – Before cooking, make 'cauliflower spiced rice' by whizzing all the ingredients, apart from the herbs and nuts, in a blender, and then tossing in hot oil and serving as an alternative to rice (page 168).

Cucumber curry

පිපිඤ්ඤා ව්‍යංජන

Serves 4

2 tbsp coconut oil

½ red onion, finely chopped

2 small green chillies, deseeded
    and finely chopped

20g garlic, peeled and thinly sliced

1 tsp sea salt

350g Lebanese short cucumber,
    trimmed, peeled and
    cut in half lengthways

½ tsp cumin seeds

½ tsp fenugreek seeds

½ tsp turmeric

handful of curry leaves
    (if possible)

1 cinnamon stick

200ml coconut milk

2 Ortiz anchovies (optional)

juice of ½ lime

To serve:

finely chopped fresh mint
    or dill sprigs

Serving suggestions:

meat or fish curry (pages 78–106)

Gotu kola (page 146)

This is what the Sri Lankans would call a 'white curry' (even though it's yellow), because it has a mild level of spice. The base is the same as Kiri hodi – mild, light and summery. In Sri Lanka they would use one of the many delicious gourds (snake, bottle, bitter or ridged), a common vegetable out there but they're not readily available in the UK. You can substitute the cucumber for English aspargus, courgette or white radish using the same method. You'll find if you use radish the flavour softens and mellows, turning into a juicy and refreshing side dish for a fish curry.

This can be made in advance and is fine to eat a day or so after. Do not freeze.

Heat the oil in a saucepan (with a lid) and sweat the onion, chillies and garlic for 20 minutes with the salt. Stir every so often and, if the onion begins to stick, loosen with a tablespoon of water.

Scoop out the cucumber seeds with a metal spoon. Then cut into diagonal 2cm slices.

Grind the cumin seeds and fenugreek in a pestle and mortar or coffee grinder. Add these and everything else (except the lime juice) to the saucepan with the onion and bring to the boil. Simmer on a low heat with the lid on for 10 minutes until the cucumber is tender and the sauce has thickened. Check the seasoning and stir in the lime juice. Serve garnished with sprigs of dill or some chopped fresh mint.

Pumpkin curry

වට්ටක්කා කරි

Serves 2–4 as a side

800g Delica pumpkin or onion squash de-seeded but with skin on, roughly cut into 4–5cm chunks, or 400g pumpkin and 400g squash

4 tbs groundnut oil

2 tbsp maple syrup

1 tsp chilli powder

sea salt

1 cinnamon stick, broken in half

5 curry leaves (if possible)

1 tsp black mustard seeds

1 tsp cumin seeds

2 tbsp coconut oil

1 red onion, thinly sliced

20g garlic, peeled and thinly sliced

1 green chilli, deseeded and thinly sliced

20g fresh ginger, peeled and finely chopped

3 anchovies or 1 tbsp Maldive fish flakes (optional)

1 tsp turmeric

1 tsp grated nutmeg

1 tsp roasted curry powder (page 202)

200ml coconut milk

100ml water

Sri Lankans eat the whole of the pumpkin including the skin – this keeps the flesh intact and is also a nice contrast in texture. Remember, when cooking vegetables always cut to a similar size to ensure even cooking. Use the seasoning in this as a guideline and adjust to your own taste as the sweetness in pumpkin, onion, squash, butternut squash and even Jerusalem artichokes (you can use any of these) varies hugely depending on ripeness. Try to get hold of sweet and buttery Delica pumpkin or an onion squash if you can.

Save the seeds of the pumpkin as, like the jackfruit, they are good toasted with a little salt and chilli for a snack or to use as a curry topping.

This can be made in advance and is fine to eat a day or so after. It can also be frozen.

Preheat the oven to 200°C/fan 180°C/gas 6.

If roasting the seeds for a curry topping, spread on a baking tray and place on the bottom shelf of the oven for 10 minutes then sprinkle with chilli flakes, cinnamon stick and sea salt.

Put the pumpkin or squash in a bowl and mix the groundnut oil, maple syrup, chilli powder and 1 teaspoon sea salt. Spread out onto a baking tray lined with paper – NOT tin foil otherwise it will stick. Put on the middle shelf and roast for 30 minutes until soft.

Heat the coconut oil in a saucepan and, when hot, add the curry leaves followed by the mustard and cumin seeds. When they crackle and pop add the onion, garlic, chilli and ginger with ½ teaspoon sea salt and cook for 5 minutes or so. Add the anchovies or Maldive fish flakes and the rest of the spices. Add the coconut milk and 100ml water, bring to the boil and simmer on a low heat for 10 minutes. Check the seasoning.

During this time check your pumpkin or squash and take out of the oven. Add the roast pumpkin to your sauce and leave to cool, allowing the flavours to mingle, for 5 minutes then taste and adjust the seasoning. Garnish with crushed, roasted peanuts and fried curry leaves fried, or with the roasted pumpkin seeds.

Tip – Pumpkin curry mash makes a good canapé on poppadom with fried curry leaf, Buffalo curd labneh (page 37) and peanuts. Simply take the cooked pumpkin and pulse for a second or two in a blender with a splash of coconut milk.

Peas and cheese curry

මුං ඇට සහ පන්නීර් ව්‍යංජනී

For the paneer:

2 litres whole milk

1 tsp sea salt

4 tbsp malt vinegar

2 tbsp vegetable or coconut oil

For the matar:

2 tbsp vegetable oil

2 red onions, finely sliced

15g garlic, peeled and finely sliced

10g ginger, peeled and finely sliced

300ml reserved whey, or water
    with a squeeze of lime if
    using store-bought paneer

1 tsp cumin seeds

2 tsp coriander seeds

4 cardamom pods, crushed

1 tsp turmeric

2 tsp roasted curry powder
    (page 202)

200g tinned chopped tomatoes

226g pack of paneer, homemade
    or shop-bought, torn into bits

200ml coconut milk

400g frozen garden peas

1 tsp sea salt

My grandmother lived in Delhi in the 1950s and she was the one who introduced me to cooking and making curries. My first cooking job was on a ranch in Wyoming, USA, when I was 23. I would email her back in the UK for recipes. Peas and cheese curry was the first I taught myself to make. I love the charm of making homemade paneer, it is incredibly easy, satisfying, straightforward and so much better in texture and flavour than bought. I also liked how my grandmother suggested to use an old pair of tights rather than muslin when making the cheese.

This can be made in advance, a good idea considering the paneer needs preparing over two days. Make extra and serve with Veena's aubergine curry (page 133), pomegranate and mint, or fry it and serve with the Watermelon, mint and lime sambol (page 157). It is fine to eat a day or so after. It can also be frozen. You will need a muslin cloth.

For the paneer, bring the milk and salt to the boil, remove from the heat and stir in the vinegar. Let it rest for 5 minutes, then tip the curdled milk through a nylon sieve lined with muslin (or a section of old, clean tights), reserving all the whey which drips through into a bowl placed underneath. Wrap the curds in the muslin/tights to keep them in some shape and put a very heavy weight on top (I use a pestle and mortar). Cover the whey and put in the fridge – you'll need this for your curry base.

Leave the curds in the fridge overnight. They should have formed a solid round cake or a flying saucer shape. Heat the oil in a frying pan until nearly smoking hot. Fry the 'cake' for 1½ minutes on each side, turning over with a palette knife until it has a crust on both sides, then cut into even-sized cubes. Drain on kitchen paper and set aside.

For the curry, heat the oil in a saucepan and gently fry the onions, garlic and ginger for 10 minutes, stirring every so often, then add 100ml of the whey reserved from making the paneer, and cook for another 10 minutes. While that is going on, toast the cumin seeds and coriander seed in a separate pan then grind in a pestle and mortar with the seeds from the cardamom pods.

Once the 10 minutes is up, add the crushed cumin, coriander and cardamom mix, along with the turmeric and curry powder, to the pan with the onions and cook for 5 minutes with the remaining whey. Add the tomatoes, stir and bring to the boil. Simmer for 10 minutes then add the paneer and coconut milk and simmer for 5 minutes. Finally, add the frozen peas with the salt and bring to the boil. Simmer for just a couple of minutes so the peas are green and fresh-tasting. Serve with basil leaves and a few chilli flakes, if you like.

Mango curry

අඹ කරි

Serves 4–6 as a side

1 tbsp coconut oil

1 tsp mustard seeds

1 tsp cumin seeds

handful of curry leaves and
    pandan (if you have any)

1 small red onion, thinly sliced

1 tsp sea salt

2 green chillies, finely chopped

20g fresh ginger, peeled
    and thinly sliced

10g garlic, peeled and thinly sliced

500g underripe mangos (about
    2), peeled and chopped
    into 4cm chunks

1 lemongrass, bruised and
    finely chopped

200ml coconut milk

1 tbsp coconut or rice vinegar

1 tbsp brown sugar or jaggery

1 cinnamon stick, broken

1 tsp chilli powder

1 tsp turmeric

juice of ½ lime

Sweet, sour and spicy. My favourite of the fruit curries – Green mango is a classic Sinhalese curry that can be traced back to the fifth century. As with the bone of a meat curry, the stone is where all the flavour is. So why not whack that in too.

This curry lasts for up to 3 days. Do not freeze.

Heat the oil in a saucepan and, when just about to smoke, add the mustard seeds and cumin seeds followed by the curry leaves and pandan. Give a good stir.

Add the onion, salt, chillies, ginger, garlic, mangos (and stones) and lemongrass. Stir-fry for a couple of minutes then add the coconut milk, vinegar and brown sugar. Adjust the seasoning. Add the cinnamon, chilli powder and turmeric and simmer for 15 minutes until the mangos are soft and tender and the sauce has thickened. Remove the stones, stir in the lime juice and serve with a meat – especially chicken – or fish curry.

Veena's aubergine curry

විනාගේ වම්බටු ව්‍යංජන

Serves 4–6 as a side

1kg aubergine, cut into
    thin 2cm slices

sea salt

vegetable oil, for deep-frying

4 tbsp coconut oil

275g red onions, finely chopped

2 tsp coriander seeds

1 tsp turmeric

2 tsp cumin seeds

2 tsp black mustard seeds

20g ginger, peeled and chopped

20g garlic, peeled and chopped

1 green chilli, finely chopped

15–20 curry leaves (if possible)

20ml malt vinegar

100ml coconut milk

3 tbsp brown sugar

Serving suggestions:
Rice (page 168)

any vegetable curry
    (pages 114–137)

any meat or fish curry
    (pages 78–106)

My lovely friend and talented cook Veena used to make curries sometimes for me at the Weligama stall. Her aubergine curry – or batu moju as it is known in Sri Lanka – was particularly good. Make sure to finely slice your aubergine (the Sri Lankan way) so it crisps up. This is a very versatile curry and any leftovers are great in a Tomato curry 'shakshuka' (page 40) or as a layer in Poppadom fish pie (page 109) or Sri Lankan shepherd's pie (page 84). It keeps well for a few days. Do not freeze.

Sprinkle the aubergine with 2 teaspoons salt and leave for about 30 minutes to draw out excess moisture and any bitterness. Rinse the aubergine in cold water and pat dry to remove all moisture.

Heat the vegetable oil until very hot and deep-fry the aubergine until golden brown, about 20 minutes, then drain on kitchen paper. Alternatively, you can dry-bake the slices in a 180°C/fan 160°C/gas 4 oven, on kitchen paper in a roasting tin, for 50 minutes or until smoky and charred. Turn the tray around halfway through.

In the last 10 minutes of the aubergine cooking, heat about 3 tablespoons of the coconut oil in a saucepan on a high heat. Add the onions and fry until golden brown, about 10 minutes.

Bash the coriander seeds in a pestle and mortar then add the turmeric, cumin and mustard seeds to the onions and stir for about a minute. Add the ginger and garlic along with the chilli and curry leaves and stir for a further minute until well coated. Add the vinegar, coconut milk, sugar and salt to taste, stir and bring up to boil.

Add the fried or baked aubergine and simmer until the liquid evaporates and you have dry batu moju – about 5 minutes. Serve at room temperature.

Green banana curry

හරිත කෙසෙල් කරි

Serves 4–6 as a side dish

1 tbsp coconut oil

handful of curry leaves
      (if possible)

2 shallots, peeled and thinly sliced

1 green chilli, thinly sliced

4 very green, hard, unripe
      bananas, peeled and
      chopped diagonally into
      even-sized chunks

1 cinnamon stick, broken in half

1 tsp sea salt

1 tsp brown sugar or jaggery

1 tsp turmeric

200ml coconut milk

To serve:

lime wedges

coriander leaves

Serving suggestions:

Chicken curry (page 86)

Spiced roast bass (page 110)

Gotu Kola (page 146)

I found banana curry in a sweet little book, The Spice of Happiness, *which also has a recipe for fried plantain skins. I love how Sri Lankans curry most of their produce so nothing goes to waste. A bit weird? Weird is good.*

Banana curry lasts up to 3 days. Do not freeze

Heat the oil in a saucepan and, when beginning to smoke, add the curry leaves followed by the shallots, green chilli and bananas. Fry for a couple of minutes then add the remaining dry ingredients followed by the coconut milk and a splash of water. Stir through and heat until the coconut milk is bubbling, then adjust the seasoning to your taste.

Serve with lime wedges and fresh coriander.

4.
SOUPS, SALADS, SIDES

සුප්, සලාද, පැති

Raw salads aren't really a thing in Sri Lanka, which is a shame as the produce is so good: fresh gourds, drumsticks, jackfruit, lotus root, chive flowers, breadfruit. Wild and wonderful. Instead they have cooked salads known as 'mallum'.

In Sri Lanka, local, organic, sustainable and wild are not cliché words, but considered of the norm. It can be a little difficult to get hold of these Sri Lankan ingredients in the UK so substitute and make good with what is available. Always use of as much of the plant as possible: the seeds, nuts, fruits, roots and leaves. For example, turnip tops and beetroot and carrot leaves make delicious mallum.

In this chapter you'll find a collection of Sri Lankan style raw salads, cooked salads and cold soups that complement the flavors of Sri Lanka, as well as a few traditional staple foods: pittu, manioc mash and fragrant rice dishes.

Although in the west rice is seen as a side dish, Rice and Curry is the national dish of Sri Lanka. Over twenty kinds of rice are grown in Sri Lanka and it is lovely to see it drying on the roads in season. Bread isn't as popular in Sri Lanka and harder than you find in India. A good pittu, made out of rice flour, coconut and water crumbles easily and soaks up curry like a sponge and is a popular alternative to rice.

Cashew Ajo Blanco

Serves 4

200g whole skinned
    cashew nuts

12g garlic, peeled (inner
    green germ removed
    if necessary) and
    roughly chopped

250g (1 large whole)
    cucumber, peeled
    and sliced

50g fresh breadcrumbs

100ml groundnut oil

200ml coconut milk

3 tbsp rice vinegar

2 tsp sea salt, plus
    extra to taste

300ml ice-cold water

200g ice cubes

To serve:

1 large papaya, deseeded

A cold spanish soup, ajo blanco translates as 'white garlic'. This is a Sri Lankan version where I have replaced the traditional almonds with cashews, and sherry with rice vinegar. Olive oil isn't available in Sri Lanka so I have used coconut milk to thicken and bind. In Spain, they often serve the soup with melon or grapes – I've used papaya instead. You will need a high-powered blender.

You can make this the day before you need it up until you add the ice cubes. Do not freeze.

Preheat the oven to 180°C/fan 160°C/gas 4.

Put the cashews on a baking tray and roast for about 5 minutes until slightly toasted. Leave to cool then soak in cold water for at least 2 hours (or overnight, but nuts don't like to be soaked any longer than 24 hours). Drain the cashews.

Put all your ingredients except the ice cubes in a high-powered blender and blitz for a good 3 minutes so everything is super-smooth. Pour into a large bowl and check the seasoning. The correct seasoning and texture are VERY important – you want the soup to be smooth and creamy, not too salty, vinegary or lumpy.

Add the ice cubes, then cover and chill in the fridge for at least 2 hours, together with 4–6 soup bowls.

Once chilled, divide the soup between the bowls and add 5–6 small slices of papaya scooped out with a teaspoon or sliced with a knife.

Watermelon gazpacho

කඳ ඹමඩු සුප්

Serves 4

50g breadcrumbs, crust
    removed and soaked
    in 250ml cold water
    for 5 minutes

50g ripe vine tomatoes,
    chopped

500g watermelon, avoid
    the seeds, chopped

145g cucumber, peeled
    and chopped

90g pomegranate jewels

2 limes, juice

1 small bird's eye
    chilli, sliced

2 spring onion, chopped

2 tsp sea salt

1 tsp coconut sugar

handful of ice

vodka (optional)

To serve:

handful of fresh coriander
    or mint leaves

In Sri Lanka you can find large carts full of small watermelons piled high, juicy, ripe and warm from the sun.

This is a Sri Lankan version of a classic. Juicy watermelon, sweet pomegranate and tangy cold tomato soup is a refreshing first course or light lunch with crusty bread. You can also add a few shots of vodka for an alternative bloody mary mix.

Excluding the ice, blend everything until smooth. Put in a clean bowl with a large handful of ice, then chill in the fridge for at least 1 hour before serving with the fresh herbs.

Acharu salad

අච්චාරු සලාද

**Serves 4–6 as a side dish
or starter**

165g mango flesh, chopped
into 2–3cm chunks

165g papaya flesh, chopped
into 2–3cm chunks

165g pineapple, chopped
into 2–3cm chunks

300g cucumber, peeled
and thinly sliced

½ red onion, finely
chopped

2 tsp kithul treacle or
maple syrup

juice of 1 lime

1 bird's eye red chili,
thinly sliced

To serve

handful of mint and
coriander
leaves, sliced

pomegranate seeds
(optional)

1 chicory, sliced (optional)

*Achcharu is a Sri Lankan pickle – a bit like we would use
piccalilli.*

*This spicy, sweet, salty fruit salad is citrusy, juicy and refreshing.
It's light and bright and would go nicely with a rich meat curry,
but is also great on its own as a starter. Very pretty too. You
can also chop the ingredients finely and mix with freshly grated
coconut to create achcharu salsa, which is brilliant with a fiery
curry.*

Toss everything into a bowl, apart from the serving
ingredients, and leave for 5 minutes or so for the flavours to
develop. Serve on a plate with the fresh herbs scattered on
top and the pomegranate seeds and chicory, if using.

Crab curry salad

කකුළුවන් කරි සලාද

**Serves 2 as a main,
4 as a side dish**

400g cooked white
    crabmeat

sea salt

1 spring onion, finely
    chopped

1 small green chilli,
    deseeded and
    chopped

10g coriander, stalk and
    leaves, washed and
    finely chopped

zest and juice of 1 lime

1 tbsp coconut oil

handful of curry leaves
    (if possible)

1 tsp cumin seeds

1 tsp turmeric

½ small red onion,
    finely chopped

15g fresh ginger, peeled
    and finely chopped

15g garlic, peeled and
    finely chopped

1 lemongrass stalk, bruised
    and finely chopped

freshly ground black
    pepper

150g cherry tomatoes,
    halved

25g cucumber, finely
    chopped

5g basil, torn

50g radish, finely shaved

125g mixed salad leaves,
    shredded

25g freshly grated coconut,
    or fresh coconut
    peeled with a
    vegetable peeler

From working in restaurants, everybody seems to love crab but not everybody loves to prep it from fresh. Buying picked, fresh, cooked crab is expensive but worth it as a treat now and again.

Crab curry is famous in Jaffna, a city unspoilt by tourists or the civil war, where you can find wild horses and flamingoes – very different to the rest of Sri Lanka and well worth a visit if only to try the local crab curry or seafood kool. Mangos and the Malayan café are great places to find good dosa too.

This salad is just as nice as a trip to Jaffna.

Get a big bowl and season the crab with 1 teaspoon sea salt, then mix with the spring onion, chilli, coriander, half the lime juice and all the zest.

Heat the coconut oil in a large saucepan. Just before it starts smoking, add the curry leaves followed by the cumin seeds, turmeric, onion, ginger, garlic and lemongrass. Fry for a couple of minutes with ½ teaspoon salt and plenty of freshly ground black pepper. Then add the tomatoes and cook for 5 minutes till nice and soft. Carefully stir in the crab with the marinade ingredients and take off the heat.

In another bowl, season the cucumber, basil, radish and salad leaves with the rest of the lime juice and ½ teaspoon salt. Gently fold the cooked crab mixture into the bowl and serve immediately, gently tossing all the ingredients together.

Wild mushrooms with chilli, arrack and yoghurt

කකුළුවන් කරි සලාද

Serves 2 as a main,

4 as a side

1 tbsp coconut oil

½ tsp black mustard seeds

handful of curry leaves

10g garlic, peeled and
thinly sliced

1 bird's eye red chilli,
thinly sliced

200g mixed wild
mushrooms (e.g.
girolles/chanterelles,
shiitake, trompettes)

sea salt and freshly ground
black pepper

¼ tsp turmeric

30ml arrack

25g chilli butter (page 218)
or salted butter

handful of parsley,
thinly chopped

To serve:

dollops of Laverstoke Park
Farm buffalo milk
yoghurt or Buffalo
curd labneh (page 37)

1 egg, fried (optional)

Flatbread (optional)

I love the combination of hot, buttery garlic mushrooms with the cold, tangy yoghurt and spicy chilli. Add a fried egg if you like and serve with flatbread.

Heat the oil in a large frying pan over a high heat. Once hot, add the mustard seeds and curry leaves and cook them until they crackle, then add the garlic, red chilli and mushrooms. Stir once and then leave to fry for 5 minutes until the water is released from the mushrooms and they start to crisp a little.

Season well with ½ teaspoon sea salt, plenty of freshly ground black pepper and the turmeric. Deglaze with the arrack and then add the chilli butter to combine. Cook for another 2 minutes, stirring all the time, until the liquid has evaporated.

Dollop 3–4 teaspoons cold buffalo milk yoghurt or cow's milk yoghurt straight from the fridge onto each serving plate. Add the parsley to the mushrooms and serve immediately on top of the yoghurt. For extra extravagance, serve with a fried egg.

Sambols

පොල් සම්බෝලය

Fresh pol (coconut) sambols add vibrancy and character to curries and break up the buttery richness. Sri Lankans have it on anything from bread to milk rice for breakfast.

Traditionally, Sri Lankans use Maldive fish, grated coconut and red onion in a coconut sambol. I omit onion as it tends to spoil easily and doesn't last a full day at the Weligama stall. I buy fresh frozen grated coconut from Asian supermarkets, but you can buy a whole coconut and grate it yourself using a coconut scraper, or you can use desiccated coconut soaked in cold water for 10 minutes with the excess moisture squeezed out.

Sambols also make great crusts for baked fish. Simply cover a sea bass with sambol, and wrap in banana leaf or baking parchment

Coconut sambol

කකුළුවන් කරි සලාද

65g freshly grated coconut
or desiccated coconut
soaked in cold water

¼ tsp smoked paprika

½ tsp chilli powder

juice of 1 lime or orange

½ tsp sea salt

freshly ground black
pepper

1 tsp coconut oil, for frying

Optional:

1 tsp fish sauce or 3–4
chopped anchovies

At the 2016 Galle Literary Festival I needed to make a sambol but we had run out of lime. I added orange juice and smoked paprika, much to the horror of the local chef. But once he tasted it, he said to me, 'Miss, this tastes like heaven.'

Stir everything (except the coconut oil) together in a bowl and set aside. Heat the coconut oil in a frying pan on a high heat. Stir-fry the coconut sambol for a minute to release the flavours. You might want to add a tiny bit of water if it starts to dry up. Sambol doesn't keep well so eat straight away or within the hour.

65g freshly grated coconut or desiccated coconut soaked in cold water

1 tbsp coconut oil

handful of curry leaves

½ tsp cumin seeds

½ red onion, finely diced

10g garlic, peeled and chopped

5g freshly grated ginger

¼ tsp smoked paprika

½ tsp chilli powder

juice of 1 lime or orange

½ tsp sea salt

freshly ground black pepper

1 tsp fish sauce or 3–4 chopped anchovies (optional)

65g freshly grated coconut or desiccated coconut soaked in 65g cold water for 5 minutes

135g carrots, peeled and grated

zest and juice of ½ orange

1 small red bird's-eye chilli, thinly chopped

½ tsp salt

2 tsp white sugar

1 tsp roasted and crushed coriander seeds

handful of coriander leaves

65g freshly grated coconut or desiccated coconut soaked in cold water

10g coriander, washed and finely chopped

5g mint, washed and finely chopped

1 small green chilli, finely chopped

juice of 1 lime or orange

½ tsp sea salt

freshly ground black pepper

Toasted coconut sambol

කකුළුවන් කරි සලාද

Preheat the oven to 180°C/fan 160°C/gas 4 and toast the coconut for 6 minutes. Heat the oil in a saucepan and fry the curry leaves, cumin seeds, onion, garlic, ginger, smoked paprika and chilli powder with the lime juice and salt.

Stir-fry for a couple of minutes, then add the coconut. Check the seasoning and add chopped anchovies or fish sauce, if you like.

Carrot and orange sambol

කකුළුවන් කරි සලාද

Combine everything together in a bowl and season to taste.

Coriander and mint sambol

කකුළුවන් කරි සලාද

Combine everything together in a bowl and season to taste.

More variations

Have a go at creating your own sambol by combining the sambol base with one of the other combinations listed here.

SAMBOL BASE

65g freshly grated coconut or desiccated
    coconut soaked in cold water

½ tsp sea salt

freshly ground black pepper, to taste

zest of 1 lime and juice of ½

1 tsp fish sauce or 3–4 anchovies,
    chopped (optional)

Raw asparagus and mint sambol

try with Egg curry (page 34), Fried mackerel version of Squid curry (page 100) or Wild mushrooms with chilli, arrack and yoghurt (page 152)

65g shaved asparagus

10g fresh mint leaves

Samphire, mango and lime sambol

try with any fish curry (pages 97–110)

50g samphire

50g mango, cut into thin strips

no salt – lots of lime juice

Raw quince sambol

try with Sri Lankan cheese on toast (page 66)

65g ripe quince, peeled and grated

1 tbsp finely diced shallot

chilli powder, to taste

Watermelon, mint and lime sambol

try with Tomato curry (page 40), Black pork curry (page 85) or Cucumber curry (page 125)

65g watermelon, chopped

10g fresh mint leaves

juice of 1 lime

Roast peanut, celery and mint sambol

try with Cabbage mallum (page 160), Green banana curry (page 137), Roast spiced chicken (page 90) or Black pork curry (page 85)

50g shaved celery

handful of peanuts, roasted and crushed

handful of mint leaves

Brussels sprouts and red chilli sambol

try with Christmas roast turkey!

65g brussels sprouts and their tops, shaved

1 small red chilli, chopped

Kohlrabi and brown shrimp sambol

try with any fish curry (pages 97–110)

65g shaved kohlrabi

handful of brown shrimp

Monk's beard and red chilli sambol

try with any fish curry (page 97–110)

handful of monk's beard

1 small red chilli, chopped

Raw rhubarb and ginger sambol

try with Cucumber curry (page 125), Fried mackerel version of Squid curry (page 100) and Black pork curry (page 85)

(omit the fish sauce/anchovies and black
    pepper from the sambol base)

100g raw rhubarb, finely chopped

10g freshly grated ginger

1 tbsp white sugar

1 tsp dried rose petals or pomegranate
    seeds (optional)

Pittu

Serves 4–6

140g red rice flour
1 tsp salt
120g desiccated or freshly
grated coconut

Crumbly pittu is not a substitute for bread but for rice, and is served with curry. A good pittu crumbles easily and soaks up curry like a sponge. A steamed mixture of rice flour and fresh coconut, it can also be sweetened with warm coconut milk and jaggery to make a simple end to a meal similar to rice pudding.

Commonly steamed in a cylinder-shaped mould inside a tall, narrow pot, this recipe is the Jaffna-style pittu. You don't need the mould, though; you can use a sieve lined with muslin instead. It doesn't matter if you don't achieve the cone shape – it all crumbles anyway.

Combine the flour and salt in a bowl. Gradually pour 125ml boiling water, a little at a time, onto the flour, stirring until it resembles fine breadcrumbs. Squeeze a small amount of mixture in your hand – it should stay together without breaking. Add the coconut and mix with your fingers, breaking up any lumps that have formed.

Take a woven palmyra basket or sieve lined with muslin and cover a large saucepan with enough water so it doesn't touch the bottom of the basket or sieve. Spoon the mixture into the basket or sieve but be careful not to press too hard or it will stick together. Bring the water to the boil, cover the mix with a clean cloth and steam for 10 minutes on a low heat. The pittu is cooked when, after lightly tapping the top with your fingertips, it bounces back.

Coconut stir-fry (Cabbage mallum)

පොල් කලබලයක්-ෆ්‍රයි

Serves 4–6 as a side

450g cabbage or kale

2 tsp vegetable or
coconut oil

10 curry leaves

1 tsp mustard seeds

1 tsp cumin seeds

1 small red onion,
thinly sliced

20g garlic, thinly sliced

2 green chillies, seeds
removed and
thinly sliced

20g fresh root ginger,
finely chopped

½ tsp turmeric

75g freshly grated or
desiccated coconut

1 tsp sea salt, plus
extra to taste

1 tbsp lime juice

To serve:

handful of fresh
coriander leaves

a few chilli flakes

bashed-up peanuts
(optional)

Sri Lankans don't really eat raw salads. Mallum is essentially a cooked salad often served as a side dish to rice and curry. I like to use cavolo nero and January King cabbage in the winter when in season, and hispi in the summer.

You can make this salad using any veg you have – you could use leftover turnip tops, beetroot leaves and carrot leaves with grated carrot to make variations of cooked coconut mallum. Tomato mallum is also delicious: replace the cabbage with 500g vine tomatoes, chopped in half or do the same with shaved asparagus.

Cut the cabbage into thin strips with a bread knife, or shred on a mandolin, and discard the core. Wash and drain.

Heat the oil in a wok or heavy-based saucepan. Add the curry leaves followed by the mustard and cumin seeds.

Add the onion, garlic, chillies and ginger. Stir-fry on a high heat for a couple of minutes, ensuring the garlic doesn't burn. Then add the cabbage, turmeric, coconut and salt. Stir and cook until the cabbage is just tender (about 8 minutes if you're using regular cabbage; the time will vary depending on the vegetable) – you don't want to overcook.

Add the lime juice and some more salt to taste. Serve with fresh coriander, red chilli flakes and toasted, crushed peanuts, if you like.

TIP - Depending on how old the ginger is you don't always have to peel it. The younger it is, the thinner the skin will be and it is perfectly edible.

Fried leeks with crispy onions

ෆ්රයිඩ් ලීක්ස්

Serves 4–6

3 tbsp vegetable or
 groundnut oil

35g salted butter

1kg leeks, washed, cut
 lengthways and
 thinly sliced (will
 look like a lot but will
 shrink to half-size)

½ tsp turmeric

½ tsp chilli powder

4 anchovies, finely
 chopped (optional)

juice of ½ lime, plus
 extra to taste

25g flat-leaf parsley
 or coriander,
 finely chopped

sea salt

1 quantity crispy onions
 (page 203), to serve

Very easy, versatile and guaranteed to be a dish without any leftovers. You could also make this with Swiss chard. Serve with various curries, in a cheese toastie, with poached eggs or as a base for a Sri Lankan risotto. The creamy, sweet, spicy leeks complement the crispy onions perfectly.

If using chard, separate the leaves from the stalk and slow-cook the stem for 40 minutes with 30g extra butter. Add the chopped leaves in the last 10 minutes of cooking. The chard version is particularly good and reminds me of Sri Lankan water spinach (kangkung).

This can be made in advance and is fine to eat a day or so after. Do not freeze.

Heat the oil and butter in a large saucepan over a low heat and stir in the leeks. Cook for 15 minutes on a medium heat, stirring regularly, until the leeks have reduced in size by half. If they start to stick, add a splash of water.

In the last 5 minutes of cooking, add the turmeric, chilli powder and anvhovies. If it begins to stick, add the lime juice to deglaze the pan. Add the parsley and cook for 5 minutes then check the seasoning, adding salt and extra lime juice to taste. Scatter crispy onions on top for crunch and serve with a selection of rice and curry or in a cheese toastie with Raw quince sambol (page 157).

Corn on the cob
with lime and chilli
ෙදහි සහ මිරිස් සමග බඩඉරිඟු

Serves 4

4 very fresh corn on
the cob in husks

sea salt

45g salted butter

3–4 small red chillies,
finely chopped

juice of 4 limes,

handful of chives,
finely chopped

*My friends Tim and Sanjay have a beautiful eco-lodge called
Gal Oya about a three-hour drive from Kandy, a large city in
central Sri Lanka. Surrounded by huge cornfields, there are many
roadside pit stops where you will find sweetcorn boiling in big
steaming pots.*

*Buy the freshest, juiciest, ripest sweetcorn possible. A very simple
and quick recipe of sweet, juicy, crunchy corn, fresh lime, spicy
chilli, flaky sea salt and rich, creamy butter.*

Preheat the oven to 200°C/fan 180°C/gas 6.

Put about 2 litres water in a large pan (with a lid), add 1
tablespoon sea salt and bring to the boil with the lid on.
Meanwhile, mix together the rest of your ingredients (minus
any salt) and place in a small baking tray that will fit all 4
corn on the cobs.

Peel away the corn husks and, once the water is boiling, place
the corn in the pan and bring to the boil again with the lid off
(when the cold corn meets the water it will cool the water).
Cook for 5 minutes then drain.

Gently roll each corn on the cob in the butter mix in the
baking tray so they are all nicely coated. Sprinkle with sea
salt and place in the oven for 5 minutes. Take out and roll
around in the butter mix once more. Serve immediately.

Beetroot string hopper pilau with eggs, anchovies and coconut

බීට්රූට් සලාද්

Serves 4 as a side dish

200g white dried string
  hoppers or white
  rice vermicelli nests

85g ghee or butter

10 curry leaves (if possible)

1 large red onion,
  finely chopped

1 tsp sea salt

1 small red chilli, finely
  chopped

10g fresh ginger, peeled
  and finely chopped

10g garlic, peeled and
  finely chopped

1 tsp cumin seeds

1 tsp coriander seeds,
  toasted and crushed

1 cinnamon stick, broken

3 anchovies, chopped

185g whole red beetroot,
  including stem,
  peeled and grated

150ml coconut milk

zest of 1 lime and
  juice of ½

To serve:

handful of fresh dill

¼ fresh coconut, shaved
  with a peeler

4 soft-boiled eggs
  (optional)

2 limes, cut into wedges

A popular use for leftover or broken string hoppers is string hopper pilau, a delicate side to go with a rich Beef curry (page 93) or the fried mackerel version of Squid curry (page 100). If you don't have string hoppers you can use dried vermicelli instead – make sure they are white so that it soaks up the wonderful beetroot stain.

I love the vegetable markets in Sri Lanka, with produce neatly displayed in grids. Beetroots are massive over there; this recipe is dedicated to them.

Boil the kettle and cover the string hoppers or noodles with boiling water for 2 minutes only, then drain.

Melt the ghee or butter in a large saucepan and add the curry leaves until they crackle then the onion and salt. Turn down the heat, add the chilli, ginger and garlic and cook for 30 minutes until very soft. In the last 10 minutes of cooking, add the spices and anchovies and fry for a couple of minutes, then add the grated beetroot and cook for 5 minutes on a high heat, stirring all the time. Then add the coconut milk and lime zest plus juice to taste and simmer for 5 minutes. Once a lot of the liquid has evaporated, add the drained noodles and stir for a couple minutes. Transfer into a clean bowl and scatter with dill, shaved fresh coconut and chopped egg, if using. Serve with lime wedges.

'Fried' chickpeas

කඩල

**Serves 2 as a main,
4 as a side**

50ml coconut oil

handful of fresh curry
    leaves (if you
    have any)

1 tsp cumin seeds

1 tsp mustard seeds

100g shallots, peeled and
    finely chopped

10g garlic, peeled and
    thinly sliced

10g fresh ginger, peeled
    and thinly sliced

1 small red chilli, deseeded
    and finely chopped

1 tsp sea salt

15g coriander leaf and
    root, washed and
    thinly sliced

1 tsp turmeric

1 cinnamon stick,
    broken in half

800g tinned chickpeas,
    drained and rinsed

zest of 1 lime and
    juice of ½

10g mint leaves, finely
    chopped

Serving suggestion:

Yoghurt

Fried leeks (page 162)

Veena's aubergine curry
    (page 133)

Fried chickpeas are a 'short eat' snack you get all over Sri Lanka wrapped in a newspaper cone or the recycled paper from an old school textbook. These are herby, fresh and ziiingy. Whizzed up it makes a pretty good sri Lankan style humous.

Heat the coconut oil in a pan. When hot, add the curry leaves, followed by the cumin and mustard seeds. Then add the shallots, garlic, ginger, chilli and salt and fry for a couple of minutes on a high heat, stirring all the time so as to prevent sticking.

Add the coriander root, turmeric and cinnamon, followed by the chickpeas, and cook for a couple of minutes then add the lime zest and juice. You don't want the chickpeas to overcook and go mushy so take off heat and stir in the mint and coriander leaves.

I really like the texture of this dish but for crunchier chickpeas you can bake leftovers in the oven at 200°C/fan 180°C/gas 6 for 30 minutes, stirring every 10 minutes.

Serve with any of the suggestions.

Tip – For Sri Lankan-style humous, you can follow the recipe above, but omit all the herbs and use 400g chickpeas. Whizz up with 100ml water and 100g tahini, the juice of 1 more lime and salt to taste.

Manioc Mash / Sri Lankan colcannon

මඤ්ඤොක්කා මෂ්

Serves 2–4

For the manioc mash:

1 kg manioc or cassava, peeled and cut into 4cm cubes

1½ tsp sea salt

freshly ground black pepper

1 tsp whole nutmeg, grated

200ml coconut milk

1 tbsp salted butter or ghee

To serve:

Beef curry (page 93)

Roast spiced chicken (page 90)

For the Sri Lankan colcannon:

1 quantity manioc mash

1 tsp coconut oil

135g shredded leeks and/or cabbage

2 spring onions, thinly sliced

1 tsp turmeric

Gotu kola (page 146) or Cabbage mallum (optional, page 160)

To serve:

2 spring onions, thinly sliced

1 small bunch parsley, finely chopped

Coriander chutney (page 109)

Manioc (cassava) is a staple food in Sri Lanka. Colcannon is a staple food in Ireland. You can buy cassava fresh or frozen from Asian supermarkets.

Put the manioc in a large saucepan and pour over 700ml boiling water. Add 1 teaspoon of the salt and bring to the boil, then simmer until cooked, about 20–25 minutes. Stir every now and then so it doesn't catch on the bottom of the pan. The water and manioc should slowly combine and you shouldn't need to drain. Mash with a potato masher or whisk, adding the nutmeg, coconut milk, the remaining salt and butter. You will need a lot of elbow grease as it is very sticky (I use a KitchenAid). Check the seasoning and serve with any of the suggestions.

Tip – You can apply the same method using celeriac to make celeriac mash.

Now for the Calcannon. Once you have cooked the manioc mash, heat the coconut oil in a frying pan and gently fry the vegetables with the spring onions and turmeric for 5 minutes. Then stir this mixture into the manioc mash. Gotu kola (page 146 – without pomegranate seeds or tomatoes) or cabbage mallum (page 160) would both make a fine addition to the colcannon. Just chuck a handful in.

Serve with thinly sliced spring onions on top and a scattering of chopped parsley. Also delicious with coriander chutney.

Tip – To make manioc chips, peel and then thinly cut manioc or cassava and fry in a deep-fat fryer or saucepan until crisp. Serve with sea salt, lime and chilli. Manioc chips are sold all along Galle Face Green in Colombo.

Rice

කඩල

Serves 4–6

250g red rice, samba or
    white basmati

½ tsp salt

1 cinnamon stick, 1 tsp
    cumin seeds or a few
    cloves, depending
    on preference

Rice is an essential part of a Sri Lankan meal and is more like the main event rather than the side dish. 'Rice and curry' is not in that order for no reason. You see plates piled high with white rice and tiny portions of curry on the side. When asking whether someone has eaten, the literal translation of the Sinhalese is, 'Have you eaten rice?'

Rice tends to be neutral-tasting, fluffy and dry in order to let the delicious sambols and wet curries shine through. It balances the meal both by being 'cooling' against the curries and by carrying the sauce. I like to cook rice by the steaming and absorption method (rather than draining) so all the flavour remains in the pan.

If you want to change the quantity of rice below, place your washed and drained rice into a pan, then add boiled water until the water comes up to about 4 cm/1 ½ inches. Follow the same cooking method below and your rice will come out perfectly every time.

Wash the rice thoroughly and leave to soak for 1 hour in plenty of water. Drain well.

Boil 400ml water. Place the rice in a large saucepan (with a well-fitting lid) and add the salt and any single spice you like (keep it to one as too many will overcomplicate the flavour). Give it a good stir and add the boiled water. Shake the pan so the water and rice even out. Bring quickly to a rolling boil, cover with the lid, and simmer on a low heat for 12 minutes. If the pan starts to smoke from underneath the lid, turn the heat right down.

Once the 12 minutes are up, turn off the heat and allow to stand for 15 minutes without lifting the lid. It will keep warm for 30–45 minutes left like this. When ready to serve, fluff up with a fork.

Ghee rice

ගිතෙල් බත්

Serves 2–4

250g short-grain rice
    (I use samba)

50g salted butter or ghee

1 red onion, finely sliced

1 tsp sea salt

handful of curry leaves
    (if possible)

4 cardamom pods

4 cloves

1 cinnamon stick

1 tsp turmeric

1 tsp cumin seeds

juice of ½ lime

coriander leaves

My grandmother used to make this and she called it 'spiced rice'. It is fragrant, buttery and cardomom-ey. I could happily eat a whole bowl on its own with a dollop of yoghurt, swirl of tamarind and fresh herbs.

Soak the rice in plenty of cold water and set aside. Heat the butter or ghee in a medium-sized saucepan. When hot, fry the onion for a couple of minutes then turn down the heat and sweat them for 20 minutes with the salt, curry leaves, cardamoms, cloves and cinnamon stick. Meanwhile, boil the kettle with 400ml water.

Once the onions are soft, add the turmeric and cumin seeds and fry for a couple of minutes. This stage can be done ahead of time and you can just leave it sitting in the saucepan until you are ready to make the rice.

Drain the rice and then add to the onion mix. Fry for another couple of minutes on a medium heat then add the boiled water. Give a good stir and shake the pan so the water and rice even out. Bring quickly to a rolling boil, then cover with a well-fitting lid, lower the heat and simmer for 12 minutes. If the pan starts to smoke from underneath the lid, turn the heat right down.

Once the 12 minutes are up, turn off heat and allow to stand for 10 minutes without lifting the lid. The rice will keep warm for 30–45 minutes left like this. When ready to serve, fluff up with a fork and squeeze over the lime juice. Every grain of rice should be separate and not stick together. Serve with the coriander leaves and a selection of curries.

5.
SWEET
පැණි රස

Sweet things in Sri Lanka tend to be very sugary. I try to make mine a little less so by always using natural sweetener, such as kithul (sap from the kithul treet), cinnamon, fruit or jaggery. Derived from the coconut palm, jaggery starts off as a milky sap extracted from coconut flowers which quickly turns into toddy (palm wine). This is then boiled with a little salt (to help preservation) and poured into split halves of coconut shells, becoming hard and dense with a characteristic round shape. The best jaggery is dark, soft and crumbly as opposed to the lighter, harder yellow kind that has been altered with sugar. Be careful when you buy jaggery and kithul to make sure no sugar has been added. If I don't have kithul or jaggery to hand then I substitute with maple syrup and soft brown sugar.

I like to take a traditional Sri Lankan dessert and modernise it or complement it with something old school and British. The avocado fool and lime curd recipe is an example of both a traditional sri Lankan dessert and an old British one working together in full swing. The Ginger Bibikkan flapjacks, Love cake, Watalappan pudding and Popsicles are all takes on traditional Sri Lankan sweet things, whereas the Papaya cake, Banana tarte tatin and the Mango crumble are Sri Lankan-style English classics.

Love cake

ආදරය කේක්

Serves 4

115g cashew nuts

125g salted butter, plus
     extra for greasing

135g ground almonds

270g soft dark brown sugar

4 eggs, separated

35g plain flour, sifted

150g honey

1 tsp sea salt

1 tbsp vanilla extract

45ml good-quality rose water

1 tbsp ground cinnamon

1 tbsp ground ginger

1 tsp whole nutmeg, grated

1 tsp ground cardamom

zest and juice of 1 lime

edible rose petals, to serve

For the rose syrup:

100ml water

40g brown sugar

2 cinnamon sticks, broken

juice of ½ lime

50ml good-quality rose water

Love cake is a traditional Sri Lankan celebration cake influenced by the Portuguese. The name is a bit random, which makes me like it even more. Usually made with semolina, but here I use ground almonds for a lighter texture.

There are many different recipes fr a love cake. This version is dark, moist and floral, slightly resembling a warm sticky toffee pudding. It lasts for ages in a sealed tin, but nothing beats it slightly warm fresh from the oven with some cold yoghurt on the side.

Preheat the oven to 160°C/fan 140°C/gas 3 and butter a 20cm square baking tin.

Roast the cashews for 5 minutes in the preheated oven. Leave to cool and then bash up in a pestle and mortar. Cream together the butter and ground almonds, either in a KitchenAid or by hand.

In a separate bowl, cream 135g of the brown sugar with the egg yolks and flour. When light and fluffy, add the honey, salt, vanilla extract, rose water, ground spices, bashed-up cashews and lime zest and juice. Mix with the butter and almonds until thoroughly combined.

In a clean bowl, whisk the egg whites with the remaining brown sugar to stiff peaks as you would for meringue and fold into the batter.

Pour the mixture evenly into the baking tin, and bake for about 50 minutes or until the cake is golden brown on top and slightly firm to the touch. If the top is cooking too fast, cover with tin foil and put back in the oven.

While the cake is in the oven, make the rose water syrup. Combine all the ingredients in a saucepan and simmer until the syrup is the consistency of honey, about 7 minutes. Then turn off the heat and let it stand to infuse and cool until the cake is ready.

When the cake is cooked but still warm and in the tin, strain the syrup over the cake, ensuring it covers the top and seeps into the cracks, then leave to cool in the tin. Serve with buffalo curd and sprinkle with rose petals.

Papaya cake with lime cream cheese icing

දෙහි ක්‍රීම් චීස් අයිසිං පියතුමාගෙ
සමඟ පැපොල් කෙ‌ක්

Makes I loaf cake

175g plain flour

2 tsp baking powder

1 tsp ground cinnamon

½ tsp ground cloves

½ tsp whole nutmeg, grated

200g soft brown sugar or jaggery

1 tsp sea salt

2 tsp good-quality vanilla extract

150ml sunflower or coconut oil

2 medium eggs

175g ripe papaya, seeds removed
      and cut into rough chunks

For the lime cream cheese icing:

100g full-fat cream cheese
      or full-fat yoghurt

50g salted butter, softened,
      or coconut oil with
      ½ tsp sea salt

finely grated zest of 3 and
      juice of ½ lime

100g golden icing sugar, sifted

I love Sri Lankan south coast papaya so much I made it into a cake. This is inspired by a carrot cake. Like carrot, the papaya moistens the cake and allows it to keep for days.

You can make the lime cream cheese icing slightly lighter by using yoghurt and coconut oil instead of cream cheese and butter, but I'd always recommend using the real thing.

Preheat the oven to 180°C/fan 160°C/gas 4 and line a 900g/2lb loaf tin with baking paper or a loaf tin liner.

Sift the flour, baking powder and spices into a bowl. In a larger bowl or KitchenAid, mix the sugar, salt, vanilla, oil and eggs. Beat until smooth and light.

Stir in the papaya and fold in the dry ingredients. Pour into the loaf tin, carefully removing all the mix with a spatula.

Bake in the oven uncovered for 30 minutes and then cover with foil for another 30 minutes ensuring the middle is cooked but the top doesn't burn. To check the cake is done, insert a skewer into the centre and if it comes out with just a few moist crumbs sticking to it and no goo, it is ready. If it needs a little longer cook it for an extra 5 minutes or so.

While it is in the oven, make your icing by beating the ingredients until smooth, light and fluffy. Keep in the fridge to firm up. Once the cake is cooked, take out of the tin and cool for at least 30 minutes. Once cool, spread over the top of the cake and serve on its own or with fresh papaya.

Bibikan flapjacks

බිබිකන් පැලැප් ජැක්

Serves 6–8

300g oats

200g coconut oil

135g stem ginger syrup

1 tbsp ground ginger

1 tsp sea salt

zest and juice of 2 limes

100ml coconut cream

75g demerara sugar

120g golden syrup

150g stem ginger, coarsely
    chopped

100g cashew nuts

This is a cross between the Sri Lankan coconut cake, 'bibikkan', and the British flapjack – the oats replacing the flour from a traditional bibikkan. Crunchy on the outside and fudge-like and squidgy in the middle. Perfect with a cup of spiced tea (page 195), these are highly addictive. Slightly salty, nutty, spicy and sweet. The amount of ground ginger and salt is no typo. Just go with it.

Preheat the oven to 160°C/fan 140°C/gas 3 and line a small 20 x 30cm baking tray with tin foil or baking paper.

Place the oats in a large bowl. Place the rest of the ingredients, except the stem ginger and cashews, in a saucepan. On a low heat, stir until the sugar has dissolved, about 5 minutes, then remove from the heat.

Add the stem ginger to the bowl with the oats. Roughly chop the cashews – or you can bash them up using a pestle and mortar – until they are crushed but before they resemble dust. Add to the stem ginger and oats, followed by the heated wet mix, and stir thoroughly.

Pour the mixture evenly into the lined baking tray and squash down. Bake for 45 minutes, until the flapjack is nice and golden. Remove from the oven and set aside to cool and set for at least 15 minutes.

Once cool, cut the flapjack into squares and serve. These will keep in an airtight container for about a week. I quite like to freeze a few and eat them ice-cold . . . sounds odd but the best things are.

Mango, banana and papaya crumble with coconut custard

අඹ, කෙසෙල් සහ ගස්ලබු වියළි ගතිය පෙ ාල් සමග

Serves 4

165g (about 2) very ripe bananas

165g ripe, juicy mango

165g ripe, juicy papaya

zest and juice of 1 lime

1 tbsp maple syrup

60g salted butter, softened

70g jumbo oats

50g dark brown sugar or jaggery

1 tsp ground cardamom

½ tsp sea salt

20g desiccated or freshly
   grated coconut

For the coconut custard

250ml coconut milk

1 tbsp kithul treacle or
   maple syrup

1 tsp vanilla extract

1 egg yolk

Warm, crispy oats baked in brown butter with clovey banana, silky mango and buttery ripe papaya with a dollop of cold, velvety crème fraiche or warm and creamy coconut custard . . . (pause and drool). It's even gluten-free! The riper the fruit, the sweeter the pudding will be. Please buy it from an Asian grocery or in Chinatown if you can. It will taste 100 per cent better, look nicer and it will be cheaper too.

Preheat the oven to 180°C/fan 160°C/gas 4.

Roughly cut up the fruit into small 2cm chunks and mix. Put in a bowl with the juice of half a lime and 1 tablespoon maple syrup and set aside.

Brown the butter in a pan. Pour into a bowl and mix in the oats, sugar, cardamom and salt. Put the fruit in an ovenproof dish and spread the oat mixture on top. Bake for about 30 minutes until the crumble is golden brown and the fruit is bubbling. In the last 3 minutes of cooking sprinkle the coconut on top.

While the crumble is cooking, make the custard. Put the coconut milk into a saucepan with the syrup and vanilla and gently bring to just below boiling point. Meanwhile, in a large bowl, whisk the egg yolk. Gradually pour the hot milk mixture onto the yolk, whisking constantly. Wipe out the saucepan and pour the mixture back into it. Heat gently, stirring with a wooden spoon until the custard is thickened, but before any lumps form. You don't want scrambled eggs.

Remove the crumble from the oven, sprinkle with the lime zest and serve warm with dollops of the warm coconut custard.

Banana tarte tatin

කෙසෙල් බැල්ල පනේන්නා

Serves 4

1 x 320g packet ready-rolled
    puff pastry, at room
temperature
60g salted butter
1 tsp ground cardamom
60g dark brown sugar
5 ripe bananas, cut in half
down the centre
zest of 1 lime

To serve:
single cream
sea salt

Letitia Clark (aka @puns_and_buns) is a great friend and very talented cook. She often freestyles in baking and has taught me to relax when pastry cooking, judging recipes by sight and taste rather than by strict measurements. The true 'Sri Lankan' way. I often text her when in a baking crisis. This is her delicious and very easy, straightforward recipe.

Preheat the oven to 200°C/fan 180°C/gas 6.

Carefully roll out the ready-rolled puff pastry (keeping the attached baking paper underneath) onto a 20 x 30cm baking tray, allowing the pastry to fall down the sides.

Melt the butter in a large frying or griddle pan until foaming. Then stir in the cardamon and sugar to form a caramel. Add the bananas. Let the whole lot bubble away for about 2 minutes on each side until nice and golden then, using tongs, carefully place the fruit side by side in the puff pastry-lined baking tray. It doesn't matter if some break and everything is falling apart – it is supposed to look rustic.

Drizzle the leftover sugary butter all over the surface and sprinkle the lime zest on top.

Wrap the pastry over the top of the fruit (but not covering it all, as shown in the picture) and bake for 20 minutes until the pastry is golden and risen, turning the tray around if your oven is uneven. Take out and serve with single cream to your own desire and a tiny sprinkle of sea salt.

(A cold leftover slice is nice for an indulgent breakfast with a strong coffee.)

Vattalappan pudding with stem ginger syrup and butter cashews

කද පීන්ජර් සිරප් සහ බට
ර් කජු මද සමග

Serves 4

16g gelatine leaves

coconut oil, for greasing

800ml coconut milk

200g dark brown sugar or jaggery

1 tsp grated nutmeg

1 tsp ground green cardamom

2 tsp ground cinnamon

1 tbsp vanilla extract

½ tsp sea salt

4 egg yolks (optional)

stem ginger syrup

Total full-fat yogurt (this brand stands well), to serve

For the butter cashews:

20g ghee or salted butter

100g cashew nuts

Watalappan is an iconic Sri Lankan pudding. This version is lighter than traditional; it wobbles like jelly, looks like a walnut whip and has stem ginger syrup drizzling over the sides.

Stem ginger is underrated. I use it as often as possible and it's my secret ingredient in breakfast smoothies; it blends well and doesn't leave stringy, fibrous bits like fresh ginger does.

I recommend using 8.5cm foil pudding moulds, which you can buy on Amazon. The pudding comes out easily, just by gently tearing off the sides. This is a good one if your friends are coming over, as it keeps for a couple of days so you can make it in advance.

Place the gelatine leaves in cold water and leave for 5 minutes. Pour the coconut milk into a saucepan with the sugar, spices, vanilla and salt. Bring to just below boiling point and whisk. Remove from the heat and set aside.

Whisk the egg yolks, if using, in a small bowl and slowly add the heated coconut milk mixture, whisking all the time until well combined.

Squeeze out the excess water from the gelatine, then add to the mix. Whisk vigorously. Get the moulds and add a couple of tablespoons of stem ginger syrup to the bottom of each and then pour the mixture through a sieve into the moulds. Cool before placing in the fridge and chilling overnight or for at least 4 hours.

cont.

The butter cashews are best served fresh and ever so slightly warm so make them about 1 hour before you serve the pudding. Heat the ghee or butter in a frying pan and, when it's all melted and foaming, add the cashews and cook for 2 minutes on a high heat, stirring regularly, until golden. Remove with a slotted spoon onto a plate covered in kitchen paper. Leave to cool then crush a little in a pestle and mortar.

Carefully remove the puddings from the moulds by turning them over and peeling the fork back. Serve very cold with a dollop of the yoghurt and a drizzle of extra stem ginger syrup on top, scattered with a few butter cashew pieces.

Avocado fool with lime curd and coconut cream

අලි ගැට පෙර්ර සහ

Serves 5–6

Avocado fool:

4 ripe avocados

4 tbsp syrup (rice, maple
 or kithul)

4 tbsp coconut cream, plus
 extra to serve

2 tsp vanilla extract

½ tsp sea salt

Lime curd:

175g caster sugar

150g salted butter, cut into pieces

2 eggs and 2 egg yolks,
 lightly beaten

zest and juice of 6 limes
 (about 70ml)

To serve (optional):

passion fruit pulp

bashed-up ginger nut biscuits

toasted cashew nuts

shaved fresh coconut

coconut cream

The first time I tried an avocado was in a Sri Lankan avocado fool and I hated it. Yet I have always had a thing for English lemon curd. The two combined are one of a kind – sharp, buttery curd against sweet, creamy avocado. Top with bashed-up ginger nuts, passion fruit or shaved coconut.

A swirl of leftover curd can be used in plain yoghurt, with toast and ghee, on toasted Coconut 'Scotch' pancakes (page 46), vanilla ice cream, or in a lime curd pavlova.

First make the curd. Put the sugar and butter in a bowl over a pan of simmering water (make sure it doesn't touch the water). Don't overheat otherwise the eggs will curdle. Stir continuously with a wooden spoon until the mixture melts, then add the eggs and yolks with the lime zest and juice. Cook slowly until the mixture thickens enough to coat the back of the spoon, about 15–20 minutes. Don't worry if it looks like it won't set. It will.

Push the thickened mixture through a nylon sieve and pour into warm, dry sterilised jars (see page 220). When cold, refrigerate for up to 2 weeks and, once opened, eat within 4 days. The curd is nice warm but tastes more limey and is thicker when cold.

While the curd is cooling, make the avocado fool. You will need a high-powered blender; alternatively, you can make by hand but you will get a less creamy consistency. Cut the avocados in half lengthways and remove the stones. Scoop the flesh from the shells into a Magimix or Nutribullet. Add the syrup, coconut cream, vanilla and salt. Whizz up then taste. If it needs more of something you can add at this point. Spoon into a glasses, top with an even layer of curd, a tablespoon of coconut cream per serving and any of the optional toppings.

Popsicles
අයිස් පතාප්

Makes 4 pops per recipe

Woodapple Pops:

4 popsicle sticks

200ml double cream

100ml coconut cream

50g icing sugar, sifted

300ml tinned woodapple purée

desiccated coconut
 (optional), to serve

Faluda Pops:

4 popsicle sticks

300g fresh raspberries

3 tbsp rose water syrup

200ml double cream

100ml coconut cream

70g icing sugar, sifted

1 tbsp vanilla extract

Kithul and salted cashew magnums:

4 popsicle sticks

75g cashew nuts

½ tsp sea salt

200ml double cream

100ml coconut cream

130g kithul treacle or maple syrup

These popsicles are based on popular drinks. The magnum, for example, is inspired by 'Kithul nuts ice cream' at an ice cream shop called Rio. I'd recommend Silikomart silicone ice cream moulds (available on Amazon); I've found these work best when removing the ices. The popsicles keep well in the freezer for about a month.

Woodapple Pops

Whisk the double cream and coconut cream with the icing sugar until it forms soft peaks, then fold in the woodapple purée. Spoon into the popsicle moulds and place the stick inside the mix. Cover with desiccated coconut if you want for texture. Spoon any leftovers into an airtight container. Freeze overnight.

Faluda Pops

Blend the raspberries with the rose water syrup in a blender. Whisk the double cream and coconut cream with the icing sugar and vanilla until it forms soft peaks, then fold in the raspberry-rose purée. Spoon into the popsicle moulds and place the stick inside the mix. Spoon any leftovers into an airtight container. Freeze overnight.

Kithul and salted cashew magnums

Preheat the oven to 180°C/fan 160°C/gas 4. Put the cashews on a baking tray, sprinkle with the salt and roast for 4 minutes. Allow to cool completely, then blitz into coarse crumbs in a blender.

Whisk the double cream and coconut cream with the syrup until it forms soft peaks. Spoon into the popsicle moulds, place the stick inside the mix and then layer the crushed cashews on top. Spoon any leftovers into an airtight container with any extra cashews on. Freeze the magnums overnight.

Cinnamon meringue, roast bananas and saffron cream

කහ 'කිරි ටෝෆි' බටර් සහ කුංකුම ක්‍රීම් දි කසෙලේ සමග කුරුඳු මෙරිංගු

A Sri Lankan style pavlova. The meringue gives texture rather than sweetness as it is slightly salty, tastes like cinnamon toast and melts on your tongue like prawn cocktail Skips.

Serves 4–6

For the cinnamon meringues:

5 egg whites

1 tsp sea salt

150g caster sugar

130g dark brown soft
sugar or jaggery

1 tsp ground cinnamon

For the saffron cream:

250ml double cream

200ml coconut cream

50g icing sugar

zest of 1 lime

1 tsp turmeric

pinch of saffron strands

For the roast bananas:

1½ tbsp brown sugar

1 tsp sea salt

1½ tbsp coconut oil or butter,
heated and cooled

6 medium bananas

To serve:

Gold leaf (optional – if you
want to pimp it up)

First make the meringue. Pre-heat the oven to 150°C/fan 130°C/gas 2. Whisk the egg whites and salt to form soft peaks. Whisk in the sugars and cinnamon gradually, a spoonful at a time, and continue whisking until stiff glossy peaks are formed. Spread the meringue mixture evenly onto a greased and lined baking tray and cook for about 1 hour 10 minutes or until the meringue is beginning to darken and crisp. Remove and check the undersides are hard to the touch. If not then continue cooking for another 5–10 minutes.

Meanwhile, make the saffron cream. Whip the double cream and coconut cream into soft peaks. Sift in the icing sugar and combine with the lime zest, turmeric and saffron strands. Set aside in the fridge.

For the roast bananas, line a baking tray with baking paper and spread the brown sugar, salt and coconut oil or butter evenly across it. Cut the bananas into long, thin, diagonal strips and place on the lined tray. This can sit while you wait for your meringue to finish.

Once your meringue is ready, turn up the heat to 230°C/fan 210°C/gas 8 and roast the bananas for 20 minutes until caramelised. Leave to cool completely.

To serve, layer the meringue with the saffron cream and roast bananas, and then sprinkle over a bit of gold leaf, if you like.

Roast pineapple/jack/mango

රෝස් ජැක්

Serves 2

45g salted butter or ghee

50g kithul treacle or maple syrup

1 ripe and juicy pineapple/450g
jackfruit bulbs/2 medium-
sized mangos

To serve:

Buffalo curd labneh (page
37) or crème fraîche

Pineapple, chilli and salt are sold all over the streets of Sri Lanka wrapped up in little plastic bags. The cult snack's flavours are instensified when roasted on the grill, which changes its texture and sweetness. Along with the mango or jackfruit, it turns a wonderfully bright yellow and becomes a sublime sauce when roasted with the butter and treacle. Contrasting effortlessly with the hot cayenne, sea salt and cold thick yoghurt. Very easy, very simple, very good.

If you are making this with jackfruit, you can buy it ready prepared from Asian shops. If it hasn't been prepared, apply a little oil to your hand holding the jack to prevent it from sticking, then cut it in half, split into quarters and remove the bulbs.

I am British, therefore I like to cook fruit.

Preheat the oven to 180°C/fan 160°C/gas 4.

Melt the butter and syrup in a saucepan and then combine with the fruit.

Put the fruit in a small baking tin that just fits the sticky, buttery fruit so that it is nice and snug and doesn't swim about. Place in the oven and roast for 15 minutes or so until the jack begins to brown.

Serve hot with chilled Buffalo curd labneh or crème fraîche.

6
DRINKS
බීම වර්ග

Exploring the tea estates around Ella and Nuwara Elya is a must when visiting Sri Lanka. The journey to and from Kandy is truly spectacular. The country is the world's third largest distributer of tea, and it is claimed to be the only single-origin tea in the world (as opposed to multi-origin tea). Ceylon tea is handpicked by women in brightly coloured orange saris with woven baskets (made from coconut husks) on their backs, and is the drink of choice in Sri Lanka, served with plenty of milk and sugar and poured from a height to make it nice and frothy.

King coconut juice (tambili), a natural energy drink, is very popular too – you can't go far without bumping into a vendor on the side of the road shaded by one of the many palm trees.

Other drinks of choice include fresh juices, which tend to have a little salt to replenish salt lost from the body in the heat. Warming drinks are soothing and milky to fend off spicy curry. Faluda, nelli cordial, woodapple cream and Elephant House ginger beer are all popular soft drinks. Arrack is the local spirit. Fresh toddy (fermented coconut palm sap) is made every morning at dawn; toddy tappers climb the palm trees along the coastlines of Sri Lanka and harvest the palm sap from unopened coconut flowers. Every tree can provide up to two litres of this stuff a day, and you can drink it very cheaply in toddy shacks in the jungle.

Juices

Ulpotha is a very special eco-village deep in the jungle of Sri Lanka with amazing food cooked in clay pots on open fires and delicious fresh fruit juices. There I ate the most amazing food and drank the most delicious fresh fruit juices. A little salt brings out the natural sweetness of the fruit and replenishes salt lost from the body in hot weather.

Serves 2

300g fresh papaya, cold from the
    fridge, seeds removed
juice of 1 lime
pinch of sea salt
2 tsp maple of kithul syrup
200ml cold water
4–5 ice cubes, crushed, to serve

Papaya, lime and salt

Put everything except the ice into a juicer if you have one or a high-powered blender. Serve with the ice.

Serves 2

400g fresh, juicy, ripe pineapple,
    core discarded and
    cut into chunks
200ml cold water
juice of 2 limes
10g fresh ginger, peeled
    and chopped
¼ tsp turmeric
¼ tsp cayenne pepper
1 tbsp maple syrup or
    kithul treacle
splash of coconut milk (optional)
3–4 ice cubes, to serve

Pineapple, ginger and cayenne

Put everything except the ice into a juicer if you have one or a high-powered blender. Add more lime juice or maple syrup to taste and serve with the ice. Add the coconut milk if you want. Like a spicy piña colada.

Watermelon, lime and mint

300g fresh watermelon, cold from
    the fridge, seeds removed

juice of 1 lime

3–4 ice cubes, to serve

handful of mint leaves, to serve

Put everything except the ice into a juicer if you have one or a high-powered blender. Serve with the ice and mint leaves. Very nice with prosecco: one part watermelon juice to two parts prosecco.

Ginger and jaggery beer

ඉඟුරු සහ හකුරු බියර්

Serves 4–6

120g fresh ginger, peeled

300ml lime juice

1 tsp cayenne pepper

½ tsp sea salt

200g soft brown sugar or jaggery

500ml soda water

ice cubes, to serve

Elephant House ginger beer (EGB) has been a cult drink in Sri Lanka since 1896. This is my homemade version – fiery and sweet. I love gallons after a bike ride in the rice paddies along the south coast of Sri Lanka.

Bash the ginger in a pestle and mortar or whizz in a blender. Then add the lime juice to form a paste. Put the paste into a saucepan with 400ml water, the cayenne, salt and sugar. Slowly bring to the boil and then simmer for 15 minutes on a low heat. Leave to cool and infuse overnight. Strain through a muslin cloth and put the syrup into a jug with the soda water and lots of ice.

Cinnamon bullet-proof 'kopi'

සහ හකුරු බියර්

Serves 2

2 shots espresso

2 tsp good-quality butter,
    preferably Ampersand
    cultured butter

2tsp raw coconut oil

1 tsp ground cinnamon

2 tsp maple syrup or kithul treacle

If you haven't tried Grant Harrington's cultured butter then you should. Cultured butter is extremely good for you and tastes far superior to the average spread. This recipe is to celebrate Grant's butter and Sri Lanka's native spice, cinnamon. It is rich and satisfying after a large meal when you can't fit in pudding.

Make the espresso and pour into a saucepan with 1 tablepoon of water, slowly bring up to boil whisking in the rest of the ingredients. Take off the heat and pour into two espresso cups. Get ready to feel super-energetic.

For a creamier consistency, leave to cool for a bit and then blend in a high-powered blender. For an iced version, blend with a handful of ice.

Spiced tea / Hot chocolate

Serves 2

500ml dairy or cashew milk

½ tsp ground green cardamom

1 tsp freshly ground black pepper

¼ tsp ground cloves

½ tsp fennel seeds, toasted
and ground

1 tsp nutmeg, grated

¼ tsp ground ginger

1 tsp ground cinnamon

2 tbsp maple syrup or
kithul treacle

1 tsp of good-quality rose
water (optional)

1 Dilmah Pure Ceylon teabag
or 50g good-quality dark
chocolate (minimum
70% cocoa solids),
broken into pieces

My wonderful friend Hen runs Why house – a sweet boutique villa near Galle. She and Why are warm, welcoming and cosy, just like this tea. I like to use cashew milk as dairy milk in Sri Lanka tends to be long life and is more 'Sri Lankan-style' than soy or almond. Use a tablespoon less of kithul for the hot choc and adjust the spices to your own taste

Put the milk in a saucepan and bring slowly to the boil with the spices, syrup, rose water, if using, and tea or chocolate pieces. Whisk continuously until the chocolate is melted or the tea is a good strong colour. If brewing tea, leave to infuse for 3 minutes before sieving.

Create a froth by confidently pouring the saucepan from a height into a mug – I love to watch the locals skilfully doing this.

Tip – Use leftover spiced tea to stir into oat porridge. Alternatively, on a hot day you can add a couple of ice cubes to either spiced tea or hot chocolate and blend in a high-powered blender.

Proper lime and soda

නිසි දෙහි සහ සෝඩා

Serves 4

For the lime soda:

juice of 2 limes (about 60ml)

¼ tsp sea salt

4–5 large ice cubes

200ml cold soda or water

3–4 tbsp lime or rose
    syrup (see below)

For the lime syrup:

200ml water

200g white sugar

pinch of sea salt

juice of 5 limes

1 small red chilli

For the rose syrup:

200ml water

200g white sugar

2 cinnamon sticks, broken

1 tbsp dried rose petals

juice and peel of 4 limes

50ml good-quality rose water

Fresh lime juice and soda are sold everywhere on the streets of Sri Lanka – you stand and drink then return the plastic cup.

Sri Lankan limes are much smaller and harder than the ones you find in the UK, so taste this recipe as you go and adjust lime juice to taste. Here I've also included a variation using rose syrup. It goes very well with lamb Biryani (page 94).

First make the lime syrup. Combine the water, sugar and salt in a pan, bring to the boil then simmer for 5 minutes on a low heat until the syrup thickens, stirring occasionally so as not to burn the edges. Then add the lime juice and whole red chilli and cook for another 5 minutes. Leave to cool completely.

To make the rose syrup, put the water, sugar, cinnamon, lime peel and rose petals in a pan and bring to the boil. Simmer for 5 minutes then add the lime juice and rose water and simmer for another 5 minutes. Leave to cool completely. At this point put 4 large glasses in the fridge to chill.

Once cool, strain the syrup in a sieve. Get the cold glasses from the fridge and add the lime soda ingredients plus the syrup of your choice. Stir and add a shot of your favourite spirit, if desired.

Turmeric latté

කහ කෝපි

Serves 2

500g milk

1 tsp turmeric

1 tsp ground ginger or
       20g stem ginger

1 tsp whole nutmeg, grated

½ tsp cayenne pepper

2 tsp coconut oil

2 tbsp kithul treacle or honey

For iced latté

1 banana

Handful of ice

I sometimes get confused with Arthur's Seat in Edinburgh and Adam's Peak in Sri Lanka. Often calling one or the other Arthur's Peak or Adam's Seat . . .

This doesn't hail from Sri Lanka but is something I am addicted to. It's comforting, warm, feel-good and caffeine-free. I would highly recommend making a brew after a long walk down from a well-known mountain when your legs are like jelly and you feel like a champion.

Combine everything in a blender until smooth and frothy, then heat in a saucepan and slowly bring to the boil. Adjust the sweetness or spicy heat to suit your own taste and serve warm.

For an iced version, blend with the banana and ice cubes for a spicy wake-up smoothie.

7.

EXTRAS

අමතර සේවාවන්

Dressings, pickles, sauces and chutneys are almost my favourite part of a meal and can really bring everything together. In Sri Lanka, beautiful handmade pickles are readily available on the stalls alongside Galle Face Green – an urban park opposite the seafront in Colombo.

Ambarella, papaya, woodapple and malay pickle are a few of my favourites, eaten alongside fried foods. Skye Gyngell calls these finishing touches 'top hats': a sauce or mayo; a sweet-salty pickle or a sour chutney, bringing together a dish and tarting it up.

Not every extra in this book is traditional to Sri Lanka, but I always have the country in mind and use its flavours – such as tamarind, limes, chilli and cinnamon.

Roasted curry powder

කහ කරෝපි

Makes 1 x 500ml jar

1 tbsp uncooked rice (optional)

3 tbsp coriander seeds

2 tbsp cumin seeds

2 cinnamon sticks

2 tbsp fennel seeds

1 tbsp black mustard seeds

2 tsp black peppercorns

2 tsp fenugreek seeds

1 tsp whole cloves

2 tsp cardamom pods

1 tsp turmeric

1 tsp chilli powder

Sri Lankans tend to use 'raw' curry powder for vegetable dishes and 'roasted' for meat and fish. Just to make things easier, I make a big supply of roasted and use for all my curries. Try to always make your own curry powder and never buy. It's like comparing instant coffee to freshly ground roasted beans. If you are feeling really fanatical, dry-roast the spices separately as they toast at different rates, or keep a close eye on them and the heat low. You don't want to burn them or your curry will taste bitter. Cooking is about listening just as much as it is about seeing and smelling. When they are ready, the toasting spice smells will start to seep out of the seeds and you will hear a slight crackle of the turning spice.

This lasts up to 3 months if kept in a airtight glass jar. You can also use it as a dry spice mix for roast quail, chicken or poussin; or add a little water and turn into a curry paste. You will need a spice grinder, old coffee grinder or a pestle and mortar.

Gently dry-roast the whole spices and rice, if using, in batches in a large frying pan on a medium heat for about 2–3 minutes until they start to colour and before the pan starts to smoke. Immediately pour the toasted spices on a cool plate or bowl or they will carry on cooking.

Alternatively, you could toast them in the oven at 160°C/fan 140°C/gas 3 for 6 minutes. Whatever you do – please don't let them burn.

Cool and pound in a pestle and mortar – a great meditation while smelling the intoxicating aroma – or use a spice grinder/old coffee grinder. Once you have a fine powder, stir in the turmeric and chilli powder.

Store in a dry glass jar with a tight-fitting lid.

Curry Toppings

A curry feast is all about the balance of flavours; the variety of textures and colours; and intriguing all the senses. Try Crispy onions wth Fried leeks (page 162); Crushed poppadom with creamy Chicken curry (page 86); Butter cashews with fragrant Mango curry (page 132); and bright pink pomegranate jeweels with a rich Black pork curry (page 85).

Be as free as you like and experiment with your curry toppings.

CRISPY

Serves 4–6

5 large banana shallots,
    sliced into fine rounds

200ml rapeseed or vegetable oil

Crispy Onions

Pour the oil into a large saucepan, add the shallots and turn to a medium heat. Fry the shallots gently, making sure the heat does not go over 160°C/fan 140°C/gas 3, and stir from time to time to make sure they are cooking evenly. Once they are golden (this should take about 20 minutes from start to finish), remove from the pan with a slotted spoon and place on kitchen paper. Toss around to make sure the oil has been absorbed and sprinkle with 1 tsp sea salt. You can keep the leftover 'shallot oil' for flavouring rice and vegetables.

Store in an airtight container lined with fresh kitchen paper until ready to use.

Serves 4–6

100g poppadom

Crushed poppadom

Crush your poppadoms using a pestle and mortar, stopping before they resemble dust so that you maintain some nice spiky shards.

Serves 4–6

400g tin of unsalted
    chickpeas

2 tbsp sesame oil or
    gingerlily oil

1 tsp cumin seed

½ tsp sea salt

¼ tsp chilli powder

½ tsp turmeric

black pepper to taste

Crunchy chickpeas

Preheat the oven to 200°C/fan 180°C/gas 6 and line a baking tray with baking paper. Drain the chickpeas in a colander, rinse and shake dry. Place them in a bowl with the rest of the ingredients and mix well so evenly coated. Spread the chickpeas on the baking tray and bake in the oven for 30 minutes until crisp, shaking the tray every 10 minutes to prevent them from burning. They will pop every so often like popcorn.

NUTTY

Serves 4–6

100g almonds

Toasted flaked almonds

Pre-heat the oven to 180°C/fan 160°C/gas 4 and line a baking tray with foil or baking parchment. Spread out the flaked almonds on the baking tray and toast in the oven for 3 minutes until golden.

Serves 4–6

100g cashews OR peanuts

2tbsp ghee or salted butter

Butter cashews / peanuts

Melt the ghee or butter in a frying pan over a medium heat. When the ghee or butter begins to brown, add the cashews and cook for 2 minutes, stirring regularly until golden.

Serves 4–6

1 hairy coconut

Toasted coconut

Pre-heat the oven to 180°C/fan 160°C/gas 4 and line a baking tray with foil or baking parchment. Crack the coconut and peel the flesh into ribbons with a peeler. Transfer to the baking tray and toast in the oven for 3 minutes until golden.

COOL / FRESH

∨

Cucumber, finely chopped
Chopped mint
Chopped coriander
Lime wedges
Yoghurt

SPICY

∨

Chilli flakes

SWEET

∨

Raisins
Chopped mango

COLOUR

∨

Pomegranate jewels
Dried rose
Gold leaf

Coconut oil and lime mayo

කහ කරපි

Makes 1 small bowl

pinch of saffron threads
80g coconut oil
3 egg yolks
¼ tsp mustard powder
zest and juice of 1 lime
½ tsp turmeric
1 tsp sea salt
170ml groundnut oil

In Sri Lanka I make mayonnaise with coconut oil. In the UK, it's more challenging as it firms up when cold. By gently heating the oil and cooling slightly, it is possible – hurray!

Put the saffron threads in a small bowl with a tablespoon of warm water and leave to steep for 5 minutes.

Slowly heat the coconut oil in small pan and leave to cool in a measuring jug. Meanwhile, get a large bowl and add the egg yolks, mustard powder, lime zest and juice, turmeric and salt. Mix with a whisk, and slowly add the groundnut oil, then – also slowly so that it doesn't split – the coconut oil and saffron water, whisking all the time. Once the oil is combined, check the seasoning – you might need more lime juice or salt. Keep in a cool place, but don't put in the fridge as the coconut oil will make it set to a butter-like consistency.

Tip – You can use the leftover egg whites for Cinnamon meringue (page 186).

Lunumiris mayo

කහ කරපි

Makes 1 small bowl

1 quantity coconut oil and lime
    mayo, omitting the saffron
1 quantity Lunumiris (page 32)
1 tsp paprika
1 tbsp kithul treacle or
    maple syrup

Stir the lunumiris into the mayo and add the paprika and syrup. Season to taste but should be good as is.

Roast cashew aioli

කහ කජෝජි

Serves 4–6 as a side

125g cashew nuts

5g fresh garlic, peeled

150g Coconut oil and lime mayo (page 206), omitting the turmeric and saffron

During a recent trip to Sri Lanka I was determined to find a cashew nut tree. I found one in the jungle while searching for fresh smoky kithul and coconut toddy. You can also find fresh cashews and their apples at Pettah market in Colombo.

Preheat the oven to 180°C/fan 160°C/gas 4 and roast the cashews for 5 minutes until lightly toasted. Grate the garlic into the mayonnaise and stir. Leave the cashews to cool then crush roughly in a pestle and mortar – you want texture not a powdery dust, and nor do you want the warm cashews to cook the mayo. Once cool, stir into the aïoli and serve with roast fish (page 110).

Coconut pesto

පො ල් ලද්දක්

Serves 4–6 as a side

100g cashew nuts

15g coriander, washed

10g mint

1 green chilli, stem removed

100g coconut oil

5g garlic, peeled

juice of 2 limes

1 tsp sea salt

½ tsp maple syrup or kithul treacle

1 large avocado, flesh scooped out

3 anchovies (optional)

40g desiccated coconut, soaked in 40ml cold water for 5 minutes then fluffed up with a fork

Creamy, fresh and rich. Everybody loves cashew-coconut pesto. Omit the anchovy if vegetarian. Have it with pasta, hoppers, plain rice, Pol roti, dolloped in cashew soup or on a cheese toastie.

Preheat the oven to 180°C/fan 160°C/gas 4. Roast the cashews for 3 minutes and then cool and coarsely chop. Put everything except the coconut into a blender and blitz into a rough paste. Finally, stir in the coconut.

Lime and coriander yoghurt sauce

දෑහි සහ කොත්තමල්ලි යොගට් සෝස්

Quick, easy and delicious. Yoghurt sauces don't really work with natural 'wet' yoghurt – you want thick, proper Greek-style yoghurt for this, or curd. Serve with a rich meat curry, Tuna and avocado cutlets (page 52), Corn on the cob with lime and chilli (page 163) or String hopper pilau (page 164).

Serves 4–6 as a side

250g Total Greek yoghurt or buffalo curd

5g garlic, peeled

juice of 1 lime

½ tsp sea salt

2 tsp maple syrup or kithul treacle

25g coriander root and leaves, washed and roughly chopped

10g fresh mint leaves

1 small green chilli, roughly chopped

80g cucumber, chopped

3 anchovies, finely chopped (optional)

½ avocado, flesh scooped out

Put everything into a blender and blitz until nice and smooth. Alternatively, finely chop the herbs and grate the garlic into the yoghurt. Pour into a bowl and check the seasoning; depending on personal taste you might want it a bit sweeter, or more acidic or spicy.

Dressings

කහ කෝපි

Makes enough for 4

I love the contrast of fresh, cold crunchy salad leaves against a rich, warm creamy curry. I like my salad colourful with lots of textures but you can adjust to the avalibilty of produce.

Sri Lankan salad

කහ කෝපි

handful of mixed leaves

handful of pomegrante seeds

a few radish, thinly sliced

half a courgette, peeled
    with a peeler

2 spring onion, sliced thin

1 cucumber, peeled and sliced

1 avocado, peeled and chopped

1 small bunch coriander, washed,
    leaves and stems chopped

Place everything in a large bowl and gently toss at the last minute with the dressing of your choice. Do not overdress.

Turmeric lime dressing

කහ කෝපි

10g garlic, peeled and
    roughly chopped

10g fresh root ginger, peeled
    and roughly chopped

150ml groundnut oil

1 tsp sea salt

½ tsp turmeric

1 lime, juice

1 tbsp kithul or maple syrup

Lime-y, pungent and sweet. I love this in the summer as it is fresh and sings summer.

Peel and chop the garlic and ginger and then whizz everything up in a blender until smooth and serve.

100g peanuts, roasted and
    cooled (to make it nut-
    free, reduce oil to 150ml)

10g garlic, peeled and
    roughly chopped

10g fresh root ginger, peeled
    and roughly chopped

250ml groundnut oil

1 tsp sea salt

½ tsp cinnamon

1 lime, juice

1 tb kithul or maple syrup

1 small red chili, chopped

50g mint leaves, torn

Cinnamon dressing

කහ කෝපි

I try to use cinnamon often as it is native to Sri Lanka. I tend to use this in the winter as it is a bit more dark and mysterious.

Roast the peanuts at 180°C/fan 160°C/gas 4 for 5 minutes then set aside and cool. Whizz everything up in a blender, except the mint leaves, until smooth, then stir in the mint leaves.

4 tbsp sesame oil (gingerlily oil)

20g fresh root ginger

4 tbsp maple or kithul syrup

10g garlic, peeled and
    roughly chopped

1 small red chillies,
    roughly chopped

1 lime, juice

1 tb fish sauce

1 tsp sea salt

Ginger dressing

කහ කෝපි

Delicious with white fish, tomato salad and mango salad, dollop some in plain rice.

Combine everything in a blender and season to taste (depending on how big your lime is, you may want to add more juice).

4 tbsp sesame oil

2 tbsp tamarind paste

1 chilli, roughly chopped

3 tbsp maple or kithul

10g garlic, peeled

2 tsp fish sauce

1 lime, juice

1 tsp sea salt

freshly ground black
    pepper to taste

Tamarind dressing

කහ කෝපි

Sweet and sour, this is delicious with avocado and green salad or drizzled onto chickpeas.

Combine everything in a blender, check the seasoning and serve. This lasts a few days in the fridge.

150g juicy ripe papaya

1 fat clove garlic, peeled

1 green chillies

1½ lime, juice

1½ tsp sea salt

½ tsp dried ginger

2 tsp maple or kithul syrup

100g groundnut oil

Papaya dressing

කහ කෝපි

This firms up in the fridge to a consistency similar to mayonnaise and is great on white roasted fish, prawns, crab and even roast pork.

Whizz up in a blender and adjust seasoning to taste. Chill for at least 30 minutes in the fridge to firm up, cool and develop in flavour.

150g juicy ripe pineapple, chopped into chunks with a breadknife

1 small clove garlic, peeled

1 red chillies, chopped

½ tsp turmeric

2 anchovies (optional if vegetarian)

1 tsp salt

1 lime wedge, juice

100ml groundnut oil

1 tbsp maple or kithul treacle

Pineapple dressing

කහ කෝපි

Delicious on anything from roast fish to cheesy pizza with lots of anchovies.

Whizz up in a blender and adjust seasoning to taste. Chill for at least 30 minutes in the fridge to firm up, cool and develop in flavour.

Cucumber pickle

පිපික්කුා අච්චාරු

Makes 1 x 1 litre jar

40g sea salt

570ml white wine vinegar

450g soft brown sugar
 or jaggery

1 tsp cumin seed

1 tsp black mustard seed

2 green chilies

2 cinnamon sticks

3 small cucumbers, sliced
 very finely

To serve, optional:

handful of crushed peanuts

handful of peeled fresh coconut

coriander leaves

I love a pickle, they go with most things. Once you have finished with your pickled cucumber, reserve the liquid and 'pickle' any veg you like, such as thinly sliced leeks.

Heat 100ml water with everything except the cucumbers. Simmer for 5 minutes then take off the heat. Once cool, add the cucumber and keep in a sterilised jar (page 220). The pickle is OK to eat after a couple of hours but better to leave for a day or so for the flavours to develop. It lasts for about 3 weeks in the fridge but then will start to loose its crunch.

Pineapple pickle

අන්නාසි, අච්චාරු

Makes 1 x 500ml jar

2 tbsp vegetable or coconut oil

1 tsp black mustard seeds

handful of curry leaves
 (if possible)

1 red onion, thinly sliced

1 tsp sea salt

1 green chilli, finely chopped

1 tsp turmeric

1 tsp dried ginger

1 tsp chilli powder

2 cinnamon stick, broken in half

1 large juicy, ripe pineapple or
 1 underripe papaya, cut
 into bite-size chunks

juice of 1 lime

2 tsp jaggery or brown sugar

This adds zing and summer to any dish all year round. Pineapple pickle can be turned into pineapple curry by adding coconut milk at the end, see tip below.

Heat the oil in a large wide pan and, when just about to smoke, add the mustard seeds followed by the curry leaves. Allow to crackle then add the onion, salt and green chilli. Cook on a high heat for 5 minutes then add the turmeric, ginger, cinnamon, chilli powder, pineapple, lime juice and sugar. Turn down the heat and cook for 5 minutes to soften the pineapple and deepen the flavour. Taste then leave to cool. Store in a clean jar. It will keep for about a week.

TIP – For a pineapple curry, add 200ml coconut milk at the end and simmer for a further 2 minutes. A fruit curry or pickle is exactly what is needed next to a rich meaty curry and totally transforms a meal from being standard to out of this world.

Salted lime pickle

කහ කෝපි

Makes 1 x 500ml jar

12 unwaxed limes or lemons

140ml vegetable or coconut oil

1 tbsp mustard seeds

40g garlic, peeled and
thinly sliced

30g fresh ginger, peeled
and thinly sliced

8 large green chillies, deseeded
and thinly sliced

1 tsp turmeric

1 tsp chilli powder

15g sea salt

20g white sugar

1 large handful of golden
sultanas (optional)

You can use lemons instead of limes for this recipe, but limes make it more 'Sri Lankan' as you can't get lemons over there. This tangy, sharp pickle lifts and adds a little bit of sunshine to any curry. A large handful of golden sultanas or chopped tomato stirred through would be a nice addition if you were after a sweet 'n' sour old-school chutney-style lime pickle.

Use unwaxed lemons or limes if you can. If not, make sure to scrub well before use.

Roughly chop the fruit into 1cm chunks, putting them into a sieve over a bowl as you go, to reserve the juice. Discard the pith. Steam the limes or lemons in a colander over a saucepan half-filled with water (make sure the water is not touching the pan) until completely soft, about 30 minutes.

Heat a large wide pan or wok and add the oil. When hot, add the mustard seeds and when they crackle add the garlic, ginger, chillies and spices. Cook for 5 minutes then add the fruit, reserved juice, salt and sugar. Cook for a further 10 minutes then add the sultanas, if using. Transfer to a sterilised jar (see page 220) with a tight-fitting lid. Keep in the fridge and leave for 1 month before eating.

Mango, papaya, passion fruit and lime jam

අඹ,පැපොප ,පැෂන් සහ දෙහි ජෑම්

Makes 2 x 500ml Jars

You will need:

2 x 500ml sterilised airtight jars

sugar thermometer

500g ripe mango, peeled and chopped into rough chunks

500g ripe papaya, peeled and chopped into rough chunks

8 ripe passion fruit, halved finely grated zest and juice of 8–9 limes (depending on how tart you like it)

500ml water

500g caster sugar

½ tsp sea salt

Amber, golden hue vs leopord print. A thing of beauty on toast or serve as a chutney with curry. Out in Sri Lanka, there is a good shop on Reid Avenue, Colombo 7, that sells delicious passion fruit jam. At weekends the market on the racecourse opposite sells many ethically sourced, organic products and is well worth a visit if and when in the area.

Just cooked warm jam on cold, fresh yoghurt is pretty special.

Preheat the oven to 150°C/fan 130°C/gas 2.

Put the mango and papaya chunks into an extra-large saucepan. Scoop out the passion fruit pulp and juice and add to the pan with the zest of 8 limes and juice of 4. Add the water and bring to the boil. Reduce the heat and simmer for 15 minutes until the fruit is very soft. Remove any unwanted scum with a metal spoon so your jam will be nice and clear.

Meanwhile, heat the sugar for 10 minutes in the oven (this allows the jam to cook faster, therefore taste fresher).

Add the heated sugar and salt to the pan and stir to dissolve. Turn up the heat so the mix is a rolling boil. Stir well every now and again so that it doesn't stick to the bottom, until the setting point is reached on a sugar thermometer or until it looks jammy (about 35 minutes if using normal sugar, 15 minutes if using sugar with pectin). Stir in the rest of the lime juice, to taste.

Cool for 5 minutes then pot in warm, dry sterilised jars (see page 220). Cover and seal. This jam will keep for a year. Refrigerate when opened.

2 tbsp coconut or groundnut oil

1 tsp mustard seeds

handful of curry leaves
    (if possible)

115g finely sliced red onion

1 tsp sea salt

30g garlic, peeled and thinly
    sliced

30g fresh ginger, peeled
    and thinly sliced

1 tsp chilli powder

50ml coconut or rice vinegar

85g dark brown sugar

400g dried Medjool dates,
    pitted

200g tamarind paste

Tamarind and date chutney
කහ කෝපි

Sweet, hot, rich, sticky and tangy. Cooked dates make a delicious instant jam.

Heat the oil in a large saucepan and, when about to smoke, add the mustard seeds quickly followed by the curry leaves. Once they crackle, add the onion, salt, garlic and ginger. Cook on a low heat for 3 minutes to soften, then add the chilli powder, vinegar and brown sugar. Cook for a couple of minutes then add the dates, 100ml water and the tamarind paste. Simmer for 5 minutes, until the dates have mostly dissolved and the mixture becomes 'jammy'.

Take off the heat and cool slightly – it will get stickier and jammier as it does and will develop in flavour over time. This chutney lasts about a year in a dry, sterilised glass jar (see page 220). Once opened, keep in the fridge.

For the Chilli butter:

250g salted butter, softened

4 red bird's-eye chillies,
    deseeded and
    finely chopped

1 tsp chilli powder

2 tsp turmeric

1 tsp smoked paprika

15g garlic, peeled (optional)

For the Tamarind butter:

200g tamarind paste

zest of 1 lime

125g salted butter, softened

½ tsp sea salt

juice of 1 lime

Chilli / Tamarind butter
කහ කෝපි

Both of these are incredibly versatile and, along with the roast curry powder, are vital tools in my kitchen. Chilli butter is great for so many things: eggs, stir-fried mushrooms, roast sea bass, corn on cob. You can roast the chillies if you want to make smoked chilli butter. This can keep in the fridge for weeks and the flavour only deepens and improves. Tamarind butter goes with most roast white fish, clams, scallops and game birds. Even roast cherries roasted in brown sugar.

Put everything in a blender or mix with a whisk in a bowl. Store in a plastic container in the fridge. (The tamarind butter will look grainy and 'marbled' – that's cool.)

Kaffir lime and lemongrass marmalade

කහ කෝපි

Makes I litre

You will need:
2 x 500ml sterilised airtight jars
sugar thermometer

Peel, pith and juice of 12 large,
   juicy unwaxed limes
3 lemongrass stalks, bruised
8 kaffir lime leaves
   or fresh lime leaves
about 1.5kg sugar
½ tsp sea salt
50ml white arrack (optional)

½ tsp sea salt
juice of 1 lime
syrup

Bittersweet, charming, limey and old school. Not just for toast, try a dollop in warm oat porridge with a teaspoon of ghee and a swirl of stem ginger syrup. Or a little warmed up with fresh mango and buffalo curd . . .

This is an adapted version of one of Diana Henry's recipes from Salt Sugar Smoke, one of my all-time favourite cookbooks. Diana's recipe suggests white rum but I sometimes use arrack, a Sri Lankan distilled coconut spirit.

Always sterilise jam jars when making preserves and chutneys so that they last – after all your work it would be a shame to have to throw any out. I do this by placing clean jars in a 180°C/ fan 160°C/gas 4 oven for 10 minutes, or running them through a dishwasher cycle. Make sure they are clean and dry before you use them.

Slice the lime peel into thin strips and place in a heavy-based saucepan (with a lid). Place the lime pith, lemongrass and lime leaves in the centre of a square of muslin and tie into a bag. Transfer this to the saucepan along with the lime juice and 2 litres cold water. Bring to the boil over a medium heat, then reduce the heat to low. Cover the pan with baking paper and a lid and cook for 1 ½ hours on a low heat until the rind is soft and tender. This is important as the sugar will harden the peel slightly.

Preheat the oven to 150°C/fan 130°C/gas 2.

Remove the muslin bag and squeeze the excess juice into the pan. Weigh the fruit and liquid (it should be around 1.5kg) and put back in the pan. Weigh out the same amount of sugar and put this in the oven in a Perspex bowl for 10 minutes to warm through. Turn off the oven.

Add the sugar and salt to the pan and cook gently, stirring for 10 minutes until the sugar dissolves. Increase the heat to medium-high. Boil, stirring often. Use a metal spoon to remove any scum.

Cook for 25 minutes and check the temperature with a sugar thermometer. Once the jam has reached 105C/220F, stir in the alcohol, if using. (Or you can put a plate in the freezer and chill for 5 minutes, then put a small amount of jam on the plate and place in the fridge for a couple of minutes. The jam is ready when it wrinkles as you run a finger across the plate.)

Leave the jam to cool for 15 minutes to allow the rind to distribute evenly. Spoon into warm and dry sterilised jars with a tight-fitting lid. Store in a cool, dry place until opening, then keep in the fridge for up to a year.

Further reading

Bullis, Douglas and Hutton, Wendy, *Sri Lankan Cooking*

Candappa, Eileen and Haas, Harry, *The Spice of Happiness*

Chandra, Dissanayake, *Ceylon Cookery*

Cooper, Carina & Rasmussen, Ingrid, *Ulpotha: A kitchen in paradise*

Deutrom, Hilda, *Ceylon Daily News Cookery Book*

Dickman, Anita, *Anita Dickman's Cookery Course*

Fernando, S. H., *Rice & Curry: Sri Lankan home cooking*

Grigson, Jane & Knox, Charlotte, *Exotic Fruits & Vegetables*

Henry, Diana, *Salt, Sugar, Smoke*

Hutchins, Bree, *Hidden Kitchens of Sri Lanka*

Jaffrey, Madhur *Curry Easy*

Jaffrey, Madhur *Curry Easy Vegetarian*

Kuruvita, Peter, Serendip: *My Sri Lankan kitchen*

Lewin, Jon, *The Locals Cookbook: Sri Lanka*

Ratnatunga, Manel, *Step by Step Sri Lankan Cookery*

Segnit, Niki, *The Flavour Thesauraus*

Solomon, Charmaine, *The Complete Asian Cookbook Series: Sri Lanka and the Philipines*

Solomon, Charmaine, *Encyclopedia of Asian Food*

Stein, Rick, *Rick Stein's Far Easten Odyssey*

Conversion chart

Weights

Metric	Imperial	Metric	Imperial
5g	⅛ oz	225g	8oz
10g	¼oz	250g	9oz
15g	½oz	280g	10oz
25–30g	1oz	350g	12oz
55g	2oz	375g	13oz
85g	3oz	400g	14oz
115	4oz	425g	15oz
140g	5oz	450g	1lb
175g	6oz	1kg	2lb 4oz
200g	7oz	2kg	4lb 8oz

Volume

Metric	Imperial	Metric	Imperial
1.25ml	¼ tsp	100ml	3.5 fluid oz
2.5ml	½ tsp	125ml	4 fluid oz
5ml	1 tsp	200ml	7 fluid oz/⅓ pint
10ml	2 tsp	300ml	10 fluid oz/½ pint
15ml	1 tbsp	500ml	18 fluid oz
30ml	2 tbsp/1 fluid oz	568ml	20 fluid oz/1 pint
50ml	2 fl oz	1 litre	1.75 pints
60ml	4 tbsp		

US Cups	Metric	Imperial
1 cup flour	150g	5oz
1 cup white sugar	225g	8oz
1 cup butter	225g	8oz
1 cup ground almonds	110g	4oz
1 cup rice	200g	7oz

INDEX

THANKS

Emily Barrett, Cathryn Summerhayes, Amanda Harris, Lucie Stericker, Edd Bush, Issy Croker, Emily Ezekiel, Henrietta Cottam, Peter Dobbs, Michelle Dobbs, Sophie Dobbs, Cecelia Llanga, Geoffrey Dobbs, Rachel Dobbs, Francesca Paling, Kitty Coles, Holly Cowgill, The Sun House, Why House, Laurie Perry, Harriet Poland, Kajal Mistry, Holly Smith, Alistair Skitt, Leticia Clark, Grant Harrington, Alice Dewey, Tom Fish, Rose Agnew, Veena Supramaniam, Shanilla Igglesden, Jason Keable, Lily Lewis, Ellie Tanner, Nicola Grigson, Rose Perry and Everyone I Worked With At The Dock Kitchen, Ducksoup and Spring.

Emily Dobbs, after working at The Dock Kitchen, Ducksoup and Spring, was the first British chef to popularise Sri Lankan food in London through her pop-up stall 'Weligama' in Druid Street Market (hailed by the Evening Standard as 'utterly fantastic'). She fell in love with Sri Lankan food as a child visiting her uncle who lived there – when the island was in the midst of civil war and her family seemed to be the only tourists. Years later, as a flourishing chef in London, she was determined to bring the food she loved to the city where she lived. You can find her on Instagram and Twitter @weligama_ldn.

First published in Great Britain in 2017 by Seven Dials
An imprint of the Orion Publishing Group Ltd
Carmelite House, 50 Victoria Embankment, London, EC4Y 0DZ

An Hachette UK Company

10 9 8 7 6 5 4 3

A CIP catalogue record for this book is available from the
British Library.

ISBN: 9781409171447

Photography: Issy Croker
(excluding pages 29, 47, 222 and 230: Emily Dobbs)
Design: Edd Bush
Props and food styling: Emily Ezekiel
Home economist: Emily Dobbs

Printed and bound in Italy

FSC
www.fsc.org
MIX
Paper from
responsible sources
FSC® C015829

www.orionbooks.co.uk

by
BOOK
or by
COOK
COOKING
EATING
SHARING

For more delicious recipes, features, videos and
exclusives from Orion's cookery writers, and to
sign up for our 'Recipe of the Week' email visit
bybookorbycook.co.uk